SLAVERY REPARATIONS
IN
PERSPECTIVE

WILLIAM KWEKU ASARE

Trafford
PUBLISHING®   www.trafford.com
North America & international
toll-free: 844-688-6899 (USA & Canada)
fax: 812 355 4082

Dedication

To the True Victims of Slavery,
and to God Almighty, whose
grace has been with them,
as well as even the
perpetrators

NOTE TO THE READER

Work on this book was completed in February 2002. Consequently, significant developments, which have taken place in connection with slavery, human trafficking and reparation movements since then are not reflected in this work.

Preface

Mankind has always been confronted with unpleasant developments having global or near-global dimensions. Whenever such developments assume intolerable stature, the powerful states or forces of the World have rallied together to find "permanent solutions" to the problems. It happened in the case of the first and second World Wars. It happened with regard to the abolition of the Slave trade.

History has shown that the "permanent solutions" have turned out to be "scorching the snake, not killing it." The very name, " World War II" confirms this assertion. However that is now in the past, and the world is praying and hoping that a third World War never takes place. The same cannot be said of "African Slave trade II and slavery." It is already taking place except that it has not assumed such dimensions as would bring together the powerful states and forces of the day to decree a second abolition. There was however a movement in this direction when the U.N World Conference Against Racism in Durban, South Africa featured reparations for slavery on it's agenda.

Meanwhile claims for reparations for the past slave trade are assuming center stage of contemporary world history. Naturally, perpetrators and victims are emerging or are being tagged.

But who are the true perpetrators and the true victims? "SLAVERY REPARATIONS IN PERSPECTIVE" attempts to provide this answer. It also attempts to show that many of the problems facing Africa today, which inevitably adversely affect the entire World, especially the developed Nations cannot be solved without dealing with the issue of the slave trade, slavery and reparations.

More importantly, everyone, including you, has a part to play in providing the final solution. Whilst individuals are playing their parts, the representative bodies of the individuals the World over: the governments of Africa, Europe the U.S.A, Canada among others, the United Nations Organization, the African Union, the European Union, the Economic Community of West African States and the numerous Humanitarian Non-Governmental Organizations have their parts to play. As for the Black-Americans they certainly cannot be left out.

Slavery Reparations in Perspective attempts to bring all these individuals and organizations together, to act, and act decisively, so that in the end, every-one of us can say that "We Killed Slavery, not scorched it, and we are all at peace with ourselves."

William Kweku Asare
Mpraeso-Kwahu.

Acknowledgements.

The author is grateful to the publishers, whose names have been credited on the relevant pages. In cases where his efforts at tracing the copyright holders have failed, he will be pleased to make the necessary arrangements at the first opportunity. He also expresses gratitude to Mike Shola Asare, who did the typesetting.

All pictures and illustrations are the author's own creation
.

CONTENTS

CHAPTER

CHAPTER 1 ||| The Concept of Slavery

Slavery has many shades of meanings. One of them is the practice whereby people are owned by other people, and made to perform unpleasant tasks against their will, without receiving any pay. Slavery, in another form, may be said to be the practice of inducing a person to perform unpleasant tasks against his will with or without pay, without owning the person. Thus, it is possible for a house help, or, even a son or daughter to be subjected to slavery conditions by the parents.

A slave, in the ordinary sense, is the person who is owned by another, and is used by the owner to do his will. Consequently, a slave has no personal liberty. A person not owned by anybody could become a temporary slave for the short duration that another person is subjecting him or her to slavery conditions.

The slave trade is the practice of selling and buying human beings to be made the property of others so that they are used to do their master's will.

CHAPTER 2 | | The Pre-Atlantic Slave Trades.

The Trans-Saharan Slave Trade

One of the slave trades in Africa, which preceded the Atlantic slave trade, was the Trans-Saharan slave trade. It involved buying human beings from sub-Saharan Africa and transporting them to North Africa. Some of the victims were retained in the North African kingdoms whilst the others were exported to the Arab and Middle East countries as well as southern Europe.

Ancient Egypt was the first state to emerge in Africa. The formation of the state was complete by 3100BC, when Pharaoh Narmer (Khufu) unified the two independent kingdoms of Lower and Upper Egypt. Slave labour became a significant feature of the great ancient Egyptian civilisation[1] Slaves played two major roles. Some of them were used as domestic slaves by the ruling class and the powerful and rich men of the society. More importantly, thousands of slaves were used in the construction of public works, especially the great Egyptian pyramids. The Greek historian, Herodotus, has estimated that it took 120,000 workers thirty years to construct the greatest of the pyramids, which is located at Giza.[2] Most of these workers were slaves. Some of the work they did involved quarrying huge limestone blocks and using levers to lift the blocks into the right position of the walls being erected. Some of the blocks measured ten metres and weighed two and a half tonnes. Cranes had not been invented at the time. The slaves laboured at manipulating the blocks into position as the pyramid increased in height. The one at Gizeh was about 140 metres

Many of the slaves used in performing this and other tasks such as farming along the banks of the Nile were Africans. They were mostly Kushites and Nubians whose territory lay to the south of Egypt. Actually, Kush and Nubia formed part of the larger state of Nilotic Sudan, which was for a period of time an Egyptian

1. J. C. Anene and G. N. Brown 1966, p. 96
2. J. K. Fynn, and R. Addo-Fening, 1991, p 19

colony. Egypt exported some of the slaves to neighbouring lands, especially the lands of the Middle East. Nubians appear to be the first slaves to be exported outside Africa.[3]

Around the mid-ninth century BC, the Phoenicians founded the city of Carthage along the North African Coast. Thereafter, the Carthaginians started influencing the history of North Africa in many ways. They needed many slaves to meet the various forms of labour requirements in the territories they controlled in North Africa. They turned to the West African Sudan, their southern neighbours, for the supply of slaves.[4] This started the long process of the exportation of slaves from West Africa, which lasted well into the 19th century AD. The trade is believed to have dwindled during the period of the trans-Atlantic slave trade only to pick up again after the abolition and suppression of the latter.

The Romans followed the heels of the Phoenicians in establishing contact with North Africa. The Arabs followed the Romans in establishing contact with North Africa. They did so in the 7th century AD. The Arabs never left, and today, North Africa has become home to the indigenous Berbers and the Arab invaders. The Romans made extensive use of slave labour. Slaves were imported from sub-Saharan Africa and even the native Berbers were subjected to slavery conditions to produce most of the grain requirements of Rome. The trans-Saharan trade increased in volume during the Arab era. Marauding Arab groups captured some of the Berbers and sold them to slavers from the Middle East. They also captured some of the Negroes of the Sahara and sold them into slavery. Some of them, assisted by their Berber partners, imported slaves from the Sudanese states of sub-Saharan Africa for sale in North Africa and the Middle East.

For hundreds of years, trans-Saharan camel-men risked the hazardous journeys across the desert to buy articles of trade from West Africa. Of all the articles bought for export, the two leading commodities were gold and slaves in that order. The kings of

3.   J. C. Anene and G. Brown, 1966, p.96
4.   J.C. Anene and G. Brown, 1966, p. 96

what is commonly referred to as the ancient Sudanese empires but were rather medieval empires (e.g. Ghana, Mali, Songhai, Kanem-Bornu) were willing suppliers of slaves, as well as other commodities that they were endowed with. Mansa Musa, the most famous king of Mali owned slaves himself. He travelled with five hundred slaves carrying articles of gold during his famous pilgrimage of 1324 to 1325.[5]

The people of Kanem-Bornu expanded their empire to the south-eastern areas of lake Chad mainly because they wanted to capture slaves for export to Egypt and also export some to the Middle East.[6]

In the nineteenth century, Uthman Dan Fodio undertook the well known Fulani or Sokoto jihad in Northern Nigeria. The jihad led to the capture of many non-Muslims, most of whom were termed pagans, from the regions of Adamawa. They were sold as slaves to North Africa. Many of the slaves ultimately found their way into the Arab lands of the Middle East

Actually, many people enlisted as soldiers in the Fulani army with the expectation of capturing pagans for sale. The religion forbade Muslins from enslaving fellow Muslims, but like Christianity permitted the enslavement of unbelievers.

According to some historians, the trans-Saharan slave trade had more hideous features than the trans-Atlantic slave trade. It involved the sale of younger women, some of whom were under ten years. The minimum age of those of the trans-Atlantic slave trade was around fourteen. Many men were reduced to; eunuchs before they were sold. The march across the Sahara desert was much more difficult and dangerous than the shipment across the Atlantic Ocean. Many more people died in the desert than across the sea and those who were lucky to survive the trek across the

---

5.   A. Boahen and J. F. A. Ajayi & M. Tidy, 1986, p. 29
6.   J. C. Anene and G. Brown, 1966, pp. 97-98

desert became more emaciated than those who survived the trip across the sea. Their only prominent parts upon arrival in North Africa were their knees, elbows and cheekbones

The East African Slave Trade

The East African Slave Trade involved the buying of slaves from the East African Coastal regions and all the inland states beyond the coastal belt. These areas covered all parts of East and Central Africa and the lands beyond. It stretched all the way to the Zaire forest regions.

The East African Slave Trade predated the Atlantic Slave Trade by far. Actually, a Greek seaman stated around A.D. 80 that slaves were being exported from East Africa.[7] They were exported to Middle East and the Asian chieftains and kingdoms. These included Arabia, Persian Gulf, India and China. Within the period, an Indian ruler is reported to have possessed about eight thousand (8000) slaves. There were many of them in Basra as well. Tens of thousands of them actually seized Basra and controlled the Euphrates basin for fourteen years. Around A.D. 976, a Negro slave appeared in the court of a Chinese Emperor.[8] In subsequent years, many of these slaves continued to be exported into China and other far eastern countries.

The early slave traders included Arabs, Persians and Indians. The East African slave trade, which started long before the Triangular slave trade (the trans-Atlantic slave trade), continued after the suppression of the former. Seyyid Said, an Arab ruler of Oman transferred his court from Muscat to Zanzibar, one of the East African islands in 1840. He established very large clove plantations and he acquired a lot of African slaves from the mainland, who provided slave labour for his plantations. Some other wealthy Arabs similarly used slave labour for their plantations. Seyyid Said and other wealthy Arab merchants acquired a lot of slaves and exported them to Arabia and other parts of the Middle East.

7 . J. C. Anene and G. Brown, 1966.p.96
8. J. C. Anene and G. Brown, 1966. p. 97

13

Some of the slaves exported to the Arab lands were used as domestic slaves. Some were also recruited into their armies. Others, particularly the eunuchs, were made overseers of the harems of the rulers and the wealthy men of the society. Some were used as plantation workers and concubines.

It must be emphasised that a significant feature of the East African slave trade was that the foreigners, particularly ravaged the inland communities and used various methods to capture slaves. These included invasions, raids and setting up one ethnic group against the other. Some early Chinese books describe how "Africans were enticed by food and were then caught and carried off for slaves".[9]

France later got involved in the East African slave trade. She acquired some colonies in the Indian Ocean. She established sugar and coffee plantations in some of these colonies. These included Mauritius and Reunion. She bought slaves from East Africa who were used as plantation workers on these farms. Then also, Brazilian ships travelled to East Africa to buy slaves. This followed the abolition of the slave trade by Britain. The activities of the British naval squadrons in suppressing the slave trade along the West African Coast affected the delivery of slaves in Brazil. The Brazilians therefore, travelled to East Africa to buy slaves. Because of the great demand by Brazil, France and the Arabs for slaves in the latter part of the nineteenth century, the East African slave trade increased in volume within the period

At the peak of the East African slave trade about 70,000 were exported annually.[10]

From 1873, the British persuaded Zanzibar to give up her lucrative trade in slaves. However, this did not end the trade. An interesting development took place. Britain asked the slavers to supply her with ivory. The slavers responded favourably. They ravaged East and Central Africa for elephants which they killed and collected their tusks for

9 . J.C.Anene and G. Brown, 1996, p.96
10 .K. Shillington, 1989, p.252

supply to Britain which used them in making billiard ball, chess mates, piano keys, handles of forks, spoons and table knives etc. The slavers however, continued to capture slaves. They used some of the slaves as head porters in carrying the ivory from inland to the coastal ports. Some were also used to work on some of the farms set up in the inland kingdoms.[11] Tippu Tip for example, used some of them to work on his maize, rice and sugar cane plantations.

The South African Slave Trade

South Africa also indulged in the slave trade from the mid-seventeenth century. This followed the Dutch occupation of the territory, starting from Table Bay in1652. The majority of the slaves were imported from the hinterland. They were mostly Bushmen and Hottentots. A few of them were Indians. The Dutch settlers enslaved them by way of apprenticeship. They were made to work in the vineyards, grain fields and vegetable gardens owned by the Dutch settlers.

11. K. Shillington, 1989, p.252

CHAPTER 3 ||| The Trans Atlantic Slave Trade

Origins of the Trade

It was the practice of buying human beings from parts of Africa for shipment to the New World to be used as plantation labourers, domestic servants and mine workers. In Africa, the majority of slaves were bought from the western coastline, especially the West African Coast and the coastal regions of Angola. Within West Africa, most of the slaves were exported from the area between the eastern boundary of Ghana and the Western part of Nigeria. The area was consequently referred to as the Slave Coast. Some of the slaves were also bought from the East African coast. The Atlantic slave trade is also called the Triangular Slave Trade. This is because the trading networks involved Africa on the eastern part, the New World on the Western part and Europe to the North.

The European ships sailed from European ports with European goods like guns and gunpowder, textiles, tobacco, beads, rum, iron and copper bars, mirrors and umbrellas to Africa. In Africa, they bartered these goods for slaves. They then embarked on the second stage of the journey, which is called the middle passage from Africa to the New World. In the New World, they offloaded the slaves and took aboard commodities like cotton, sugar cane,

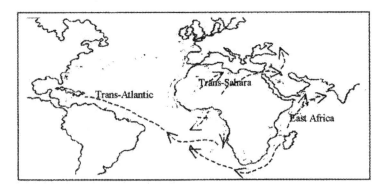

Slave Routes

16

tobacco, tea and minerals especially gold for the third and final leg of the voyage to Europe, to re-start the journey.

A number of factors necessitated the export of slaves to the New World. The first was the so-called discovery of the New World by the Europeans. As part of the 15th century voyages of discovery, organised by some European countries to find out the true shape of the Earth, and a sea route to India and the Far East, that would by-pass the Muslim controlled Middle East, Christopher Columbus travelled west and discovered one of the Bahamas on October 12, 1492 on behalf of Spain. Besides scientific curiosity another reason for the voyages was to ensure continued supply of spices to Europe, which was jeopardised by the Muslim control of the Middle East. Within forty years of Columbus' discovery, Spain had secured a vast empire embracing Hispaniola, Peru, Mexico, Panama and Cuba.

The Spaniards and other European nations, which followed later, established plantation farms to produce crops like cotton, sugar cane, tobacco and tea. They also opened up mines, the most important being gold mines. This called for a large labour force. The Europeans were generally not prepared to do the work themselves. They started by recruiting the indigenous people to do the work. The Amerindians could not cope with the work. Considering the rate at which they were dying, they faced extinction. The population reduced from about one million in 1492 to about 60,000 in 1510 and around 11,000 in 1518.[1]

To halt the threat to the decimation, it became necessary to look for an alternative suitable labour force. The lot fell on Africans. In 1441, Gonzalves, a Portuguese explorer, had presented ten Africans to Prince Henry of Portugal.[2].They were the first Africans to be sent to Europe. This first set were more or less objects aimed at satisfying the curiosity of Europeans at home who had been hearing of blacks, but had never had the opportunity of seeing some. Between 1486 and 1493, an average

1.   J. K. Fynn and R. Addo-Fening, 1991, p. 210
2.   A. Boahen and J. F. Ade Ajayi and M. Tidy, 1986, p.210

of 448 African slaves belonging to the kings of Portugal were being imported annually into Portugal. Some of them were used as domestic slaves. Others were used as farm workers. Thus by the time the Amerindians were dying from their labour on the plantations and mines, Europeans had a good idea of the African's ability to withstand such exactions. Bishop Las Casas therefore petitioned the Spanish crown to allow the importation of slaves from Africa to the New World. The permission was granted and the first direct shipment of slaves from Africa to the New World took place in 1518.[3]

Organisation of the Atlantic Slave Trade.

A fair knowledge of how the Atlantic Slave Trade was organised will help the interested individual to take an objective decision on the reparations question. The trade was a complete financial enterprise that had all the factors of production and distribution.

Entrepreneurs, financiers and buyers.

Merchants from many European countries and also Brazil were involved in the buying of slaves from Africa and their sale in the New World. The major European countries were Portugal, Spain, Britain, France, Holland, Denmark, Sweden and Germany. The European governments gave recognition and backing to the merchants from their countries. Portugal initially opened registers for them. The registers served as license for the slavers to supply specified numbers of slaves for resale. In Britain and Holland, Trading Companies were formed. Their kings granted the Companies Royal Charters empowering them to transact business and to enjoy the protection of the crown.

Some merchants operated outside the law. They were smugglers and were called interlopers. They were not entitled to any official protection and rather stood the risk of being prosecuted if they were caught.

Outside Europe, Brazilian traders crossed the Atlantic to Africa to

3. J. K. Fynn and Addo Fening, 1991, p. 210

18

buy slaves. The main areas that attracted the Portuguese slavers were the regions of Angola and East African Coast.

The European merchants loaded their ships with goods from Europe, which they bartered for slaves. At the peak of the trade the article of trade that had the greatest demand were guns and the accompanying gunpowder. In Europe, especially in Birmingham, factories were set up to manufacture special cheap long barrelled guns for Africa.[4] The guns were as dangerous to the wielder as to the object targeted. Other items battered were cheap and mainly gaudy textiles said to be inferior to most of the textiles produced in Africa, brass and copper products, iron bars, alcoholic drinks, tobacco and smoking pipes and mirrors. The iron bars, besides being used by blacksmiths to manufacture weapons, tools and utensils, were also used as currency in some parts of Africa.

The Portuguese introduced cowries from the Indian Ocean trade into the trading system. Cowries were used as currency.

The European merchants also introduced the credit system into the trade. Some historians have argued that it was the European merchants who introduced the credit system into the West African trade for the first time. However, others have postulated that the Mande Dyula were responsible for this. They were a group of people that originated in Mali. They were Muslims by religion and traders by profession. They travelled in between the Sudanese Empires and the forest states thereby linking these two regions by trade. Be that as it may, the European merchants advanced goods to their "protectors" or "landlords" who advanced the goods to their subjects for them to go inland and buy slaves for the Europeans. If the subjects defaulted, the "landlord" was held responsible and he in turn dealt with the defaulter by selling him and his family members into slavery.

Suppliers of slaves

There is agreement amongst historians, including the leading

---

4. J. F. Ajayi And I. Espie, 1965, P.248

African writers that European merchants did not embark on raiding activities for slaves. They relied on prominent African leaders to supply them with the slaves.[5] The prominent African leaders included local coastal chiefs, the elders of the communities, as well as wealthy and respected members of the communities.

The suppliers sold different categories of slaves to the European merchants. At the very beginning of the trade, when demand was not so high, they sold mainly pawns and domestic slaves. Pawns were those individuals, who had been released by their poor relations, in most cases, their fathers to rich moneylenders or any other form of lenders to serve as security until they were redeemed upon the payment of what was owed. Domestic slaves were those who had been acquired through all sorts of means, and were used to perform all sorts of household work. Some were bought; others were criminals or prisoners of wars. Some others could be notorious members of a family who had been released into slavery.

Natives were also engaging in panyarring. The victims of panyarring were also sold. However, the demand for slaves far exceeded what these simple sources could meet.

African communities engaged in raids in order to obtain larger numbers of slaves. Not even the raids could meet the demand. Africans then intensified the inter-ethnic wars they had been engaging in on a comparatively smaller scale before the introduction of the Atlantic slave trade.

Both European and African writers of African history have sought to find out whether the many wars fought during the slave trade period were motivated by the desire to secure slaves for sale, or for different reasons, such as the formation and expansion of states, with the by-product of generating war captives, who were sold as slaves. The answer is that both factors were at work. All the 17th and 18th centuries' wars of West Africa, such as the

B. Adu with F. F. Ajayi and M. Tidy 1986, p. 108

Asante wars, the Dahomey wars and the Oyo wars had these mixed motives. They were interested in consolidating and expanding their kingdoms as well as securing captives for sale. The fact is that, success at wars within the period was closely linked to the possession of guns and gunpowder, and the determinant factor for obtaining guns and gunpowder was the ability to trade slaves in exchange for them. The key to opening the door for access to all other imported European goods was the willingness to supply slaves.

Movement to the Coast.

Once the slaves were obtained through the various means mainly in the inland communities, they were transported to the coast through a network of middlemen. Many of the middlemen were native agents to the coastal chiefs. They bought the slaves from the inland rulers and other leaders. They exchanged them with the European goods advanced to them by the coastal rulers. Upon their arrival at the coast they handed them over to the coastal leaders, who in turn supplied them to the European slavers. There were also those African agents who supplied their cargo directly to the Europeans. The slaves were marched from the interior to the coast in long caravans along well-defined slave routes. Many of such slave routes are today being identified by some of the African states and marked out for the purpose of tourism. The main group being targeted is the black Americans, who are interested in identifying their past, and having as much physical contact as is possible with the past.

A few daring Afro-Europeans and Europeans actually took part in marching slaves from the interior to the coast.

The owners of the slaves hired guards, who were blacks, to escort the caravans to the coast. All the guards wielded whips to intimidate the slaves and make them subservient. The whips were liberally used. It was commonplace for those considered stubborn to have welts on their backs upon arrival at the coast. Some of the slaves never reached the coast alive.

To prevent the slaves from escaping or assaulting the guards, their legs were fastened together with chains. The chains moved from the left leg of the one ahead to the right leg of the one behind in that order up to the very last person. It was also a common practice to fasten sets of slaves together by the neck. Usually, they were fastened in sets of four. Their hands were also tied up in the night

Slaves en route to the coast

"Storage" at the Coast.

Once the slaves reached the coast, they had to be kept securely until ships were ready to take them away on the "middle passage" across the Atlantic Ocean to the New World. Ships were said to be ready in two ways. In the first place, a full cargo could be ready without a ship being at dock. The ship was ready when it arrived along the coast to take aboard its cargo. Secondly, a ship could be at anchor along the West African Coast, without the full cargo being ready. It had to wait until the required numbers of slaves had been bought and assembled by the European merchants.

Various facilities were put in place for storing the slaves until they were ready for shipment. Forts and castles were constructed at some locations along the coast for this purpose among others. Most of the forts and castles in Africa were constructed in the Gold Coast (the Republic of Ghana). They were constructed basically to protect the owners or the inmates against enemies.

22

The enemies could be Europeans from other countries or the natives. They were also used as warehouses for European goods and slaves until they were ready to be disposed off. The forts and castles were also meant to protect the European goods against possible theft by unscrupulous natives. Whilst awaiting shipment, the slaves were kept in the dungeons of the castles. These dungeons were not provided with lighting systems and they were poorly ventilated. The floors of the dungeons were sloped. This made for involuntary defecations and other bodily discharges to flow towards the lowest end to be cleared up at the appropriate time.

In some places where there were no forts and castles, some of the European merchants traded from ships anchored in rivers. This was the common practice in the Niger Delta of Nigeria. Some Europeans and native coastal slave dealers at times constructed barracoons or pens for holding slaves before transporting them onto ships. All pens and barracoons employed trusted, strong and powerful native guards to prevent any possible escape.

The chiefs on whose lands Europeans constructed forts or barracoons served as landlords or protectors to the Europeans.

Slave barracoon

Such Europeans paid rents to their landlords. In addition, they also paid customary duties. It is believed that some of the "tenants" also paid commission on each slave sold[6]

Transportation to the New World.

The slaves were finally shipped to the New World by European merchants and some Brazilian merchants. The merchants made sure that the cargo they were taking aboard was in the best of conditions. Every slave was subjected to thorough physical examination before embarkation. They were stripped naked for this purpose. It is only those who passed the test that were taken aboard.

The hatches of the ships were fitted with special decks. The spaces between the decks ranged between half a metre and one and a half metres. It is on these shelves that the slaves lay chained together in the most horrible of hygienic conditions. They lay in their urine and excreta, in darkness with access to very little fresh air for breathing. They were provided with the barest of food and water to keep them alive. It is no wonder that every morning, at least one of them was found dead, still fastened onto the living ones. They were so closely packed that the shelf on which they lay did not have space to contain one more. They were subjected to this condition for the six to ten weeks that it took the ships to cross the Atlantic Ocean.

At Destination

When the ships arrived in the New World, the slaves were sold to those who were interested in buying them. They were first sorted out. Those who had fallen ill or become feeble as a result of the problems experienced during the voyage were the first to be sold as trifles. The healthy looking ones were mounted on platforms for thorough examination by prospective buyers. They were then sold by auction. The price paid for the slaves normally ranged between $1200 and $1800 each.[7]

6. J.F. Ade Ajayi and I. Espie, 1965, p 250
7. M. G. Kelty, 1937, p. 461

Having bought the slaves, their masters took them home to be used as it pleased them. The common tasks they were put to were working on plantations, mines and domestic chores.

Abolition and Suppression

Reasons:
In 1807, the British Parliament declared slavery illegal for British subjects or nationals. In 1833, the parliament abolished slavery in all British possessions or colonies. There were many reasons why Britain decided to abolish the slave trade.

A new class of people referred to as the industrial barons emerged in Britain and displaced the former sugar barons by way of power and importance. They felt the slave trade worked against their interests and the interests of their country. They therefore fought hard for the abolition of the trade. For a number of reasons, French West Indies was able to produce cheaper sugar than the British West Indies. Many Europeans started buying sugar form the French rather than the British. When the American colonies revolted against Britain, they also started buying French sugar which they had up till then been forbidden to buy. The British therefore had to reduce production. This meant that the services of many of their slaves were no longer needed. The plantation owners actually abandoned many of the slaves to their fate.
Many of them died out of starvation. Britain, at that time, clearly did not need more slaves.

Secondly, the industrial barons wanted to cut off further supply of slaves to the French West Indies. They expected the action to cause a rise in the price of the West Indies sugar so that the British would be able to compete with them.

The barons also felt that the triangular trade was outmoded. They wanted a new arrangement whereby British merchant ships would sail from home to specific locations of the world with British goods to be traded with the products of that destination for the vessel to return directly home. Thus, British ships, upon offloading their manufactured goods in Africa would return with products of Africa such as palm oil, groundnut oil, cotton, ivory, timber and gold. They expected their ships, which sailed to Brazil with British goods to return with Brazilian sugar and coffee. They also expected their ships, which offloaded their manufactured goods in the U.S.A., to return with cotton for example.

Again the industrial barons argued that the slave trade was not making it possible for them to obtain the volume of palm oil they wanted from West Africa. The reasons for this is that the African chiefs were making more profit than they did from supplying palm oil. As such, they concentrated on meeting the demands of the slavers before attending to the legitimate traders. This made British merchants who had docked to buy palm oil spend too much time along the West African Coast. At times, oilers had to wait for one full year before their demands were met[8]

Another reason was the humanitarian and evangelical revival that took place during the last quarter of the eighteenth century. Some people in Britain started giving thought to their perception of other human beings especially blacks, their attitudes towards them and their relationship with them. Many of them arrived at the inevitable conclusion that all men were equal regardless of colour, origin, religion etc. Closely associated with this was the evangelical revival. Many Europeans started re-examining their faith and attitude towards God. They gave greater thought to the teachings in the Bible and what it meant personally to them. One teaching, which hit them in the face, was Genesis 1:26 "And God said, let us make man in our image, and after our likeness…"Another one was- "Love your neighbour as yourself" and yet another, "Do unto others what you want them to do to you…" Every one of these teachings convicted them, and they realised that they had sinned against God and their fellow men. They felt the least they could do to atone for their sins was to work towards the abolition of slavery and the slave trade, and introduce Christianity to the blacks. They could also encourage them to take to the legitimate trade. As early as the 15th century, some few but powerful church leaders had started condemning slavery. Pope Pius II was one of them. Popes Leo X and Paul III

8. J. B. Webster, A. A. Boahen H. O. Idowu, p. 78

did so in the 16th century. Pope Urban VIII did so in the 17th century. They made it clear that slavery and the slave trade were against the Christian religion and nature. In the words of Pope Leo X in 1554, "Not only the Christian religion, but nature cries out against slavery and the slave trade"[9].

The philosophical ideas of the day were very powerful and created many revolutionary changes. Some of the changes were the French revolution, and the American Revolution. The theme of the outstanding philosophers of the period, especially the Swiss-born French philosopher Rousseau, (1712-78) was the equality and brotherhood of men. Rousseau published his book, the Social Contract in 1762. The book began with the statement that " Man was born free, and is everywhere in chains". It could be seen that the lower classes, the commoners, were in the chains of the upper classes that were the ruling classes in some parts of the world, colonies were in the chains of their colonial masters etc. As for slaves, they were literally in chains. They were in the chains of their owners. The call was being trumpeted for the breaking of various forms of chains in which man found himself everywhere.

Measures taken to abolish slave trade and slavery

Slavery was abolished not only because of the changes in the beliefs and attitudes of some of the great men at the time, it was abolished because they mobilised themselves and various forms of resources to fight battles at different fronts for abolition.

One of the areas was the court. In 1772, Granville Sharp filed a motion in the court of the chief Justice of England, the Lord chief Justice Mansfield on behalf of a slave called James Somerset, to be given his freedom from his master. The chief justice ruled that the laws of England did not recognise slavery.

Granville Sharp did not carry out the fight alone; neither did the abolitionists restrict the fight to the courts. The evangelists and

9. F. K. Buah 1979, P. 49

27

humanitarians formed Associations to fight for the abolition of the trade. An example is the Quakers. The Quakers were active in England as well as America. In 1783 for example, the Quakers in England formed a committee of six to organise propaganda for the freeing of slaves in the West Indies as well as stopping their export from West Africa. The committee was expanded and transformed into a more powerful organisation called the Society for the abolition of the slave trade in 1787. The Association fought within and outside the British Parliament for the abolition of slavery and the slave trade. The fight was not easy, and they lost eight motions for abolition between 1772 and 1805. Their efforts finally became successful in 1807 when parliament enacted a law declaring the buying and selling of slaves illegal in the United Kingdom.

Many factors contributed to ensure success. Every member of the Association played his part. Thomas Clarkson worked relentlessly outside parliament to arouse public opinion by gathering and articulating stories of brutality meted out to the slaves. William Wilberforce, a Parliamentarian used the facts gathered by Clarkson to campaign in Parliament against the slave trade. Granville Sharp handled most of the legal aspects of the campaign. They made use of every known campaign facility at the time. These included, newspapers, books, pamphlets and getting clergymen to preach sermons.

The industrial barons also influenced parliament through their representatives in the legislature.

Around the time that the slave trade was being abolished in England some other countries were doing the same. Denmark had done so in 1805. United States of America banned its citizens from engaging in the slave trade in 1808. Sweden did so in 1813, Holland, 1814 and France in 1817. These laws only legally abolished the slave trade; they did not abolish slavery itself. Even the slave trade, in practice, continued and increased in many places until the British took steps to suppress the trade.

Meanwhile, a few Africans had also made some efforts to draw the attention of some Europeans to the evil of slavery and the slave trade and pleaded with Europeans to abolish the institution and the practice. As early as 1526, the Congolese King, Nzinga Mbemba petitioned the king of Portugal to stop the Portuguese from buying slaves from his kingdom.[10] Mamodu Yeli, a Muslim Mandinka Scholar of Sierra Leone unsuccessfully fought for the stopping of slave trade among his fellow Muslims.[11] Olaudah Equiano, a former Ibo slave sought to influence the British parliament by addressing a book to the Institution on Christmas Eve in 1789 declaring (in the book) that his aim was to "excite in your august assembly a sense of compassion for the miseries which the slave trade had entailed on my unfortunate countrymen. May God of heaven inspire your hearts with peculiar benevolence on that particular day when the question of Abolition is to be discussed, when thousands in consequence of your determination, are to look for happiness or misery"[12].

There were some Black Americans also who worked towards the abolition of slavery and the slave trade. Some of the leading members are Alexander Crummel, Martin Delaney and Frederick Douglas.

After the abolition of the slave trade, measures were taken to abolish slavery itself. On 28th August 1833, the British parliament passed a law declaring slavery illegal not only in the United Kingdom but throughout the British Empire. To prevent the sudden collapse of the plantations and also the dislocation of household work, the plantation slaves were to serve for eight years while the domestic slaves were to serve for four years before enjoying full freedom. Both categories of slaves were however granted full emancipation in 1838.

In the U.S.A. President Abraham Lincoln issued the Emancipation decree in 1863. The Thirteenth Amendment gave the decree the force of law in 1865.

10. F. K. Buah, 1997 F, p. 49
11. J. B. Webster, A. A. Boahen, H. O. Idowu, 19667. p. 85
12. *Quote in* F. K. Buah, 1979, pp. 49-50

Suppression

The abolition laws passed by the Britain and other nations meant that the trade was illegal. All the same, slavers from almost all the countries continued to buy slaves from Africa. African Chiefs continued to supply slavers with slaves because of the huge profits they made. Britain then introduced practical measures to suppress the trafficking.

In the first place, she stationed a naval squadron in Sierra Leone to patrol the West African Coast and seize ships carrying slaves on their way to the New World. Since it was practically impossible to call at all the ports to disembark slaves aboard seized ships at their ports of embarkation, all of them were set free in Sierra Leone. They were called the recaptives. They were added to the Creoles. The Creoles were freed slaves from Britain and the New World (mainly Nova Scotia) who had been resettled in Sierra Leone to start life afresh. The present population of Sierra Leone is made up of the recaptives; the Creoles and the indigenous ethnic populations the immigrants came to join.

Besides her own subjects, Britain did not have the legal authority to arrest ships from other countries, which were carrying slaves to the New World. She therefore appealed to them to join her in a great act of humanitarianism to stamp out the trade. The other Nations were convinced that Britain was motivated, not so much by humanitarian considerations as by economic considerations. They realised that because of the stage of industrialisation attained by Britain, the slave trade was hampering her further industrial growth. They, on the other hand, were still at the stage where the trade did not interfere with their economic prosperity. Britain used force to arrest the ships of the weaker nations. Again she bribed Spain and Portugal to give up the slave trade. She then proceeded to search the ships of the other nations besides the United States (which was too powerful to be treated anyhow) and arrested ships found with slaves. The slavers then resorted to throwing overboard all slaves in the ship immediately they saw a British Naval patrol boat approaching.

To solve this problem, the British then signed "Equipment Treaties" with willing countries i.e. France and Spain. This gave Britain the power to arrest ships fitted with equipment for carrying slaves whether or not they were actually carrying slaves. Since the United States, Portugal and Spain did not sign, those who had signed started hoisting the flags of those who had not. Britain proceeded to seize the ships of Portugal and Brazil illegally because they were weak nations. The two countries signed the treaties with equipment clauses in 1840. Since the United States had not signed, notorious slavers hoisted American flags to escape capture. The problem was solved when the United States willingly emancipated slaves in 1863 and the northern states signed a treaty with Britain allowing her to seize American ships fitted with slaving equipment. The main reason for the action taken by the northern states was to secure British friendship in her war against the southern states.

Before this, Britain had taken another practical step of compelling West African coastal chiefs to allow the Naval patrol boats to seize slavers loading at the ports.

Abolition of the East African Slave Trade

The East African Slave Trade between Africans and Arabs was never formally abolished.

Abolition Of The Trans-Saharan Slave Trade

The trans-Saharan slave trade between Africans and Arabs was never formally abolished.

CHAPTER 4 | Call For Reparations.

In recent times, voices have been raised for compensation to be paid to Africa and peoples of African descent for the slave trade and colonialism. Reparations may be defined as the act of paying compensation for loss, or for damage. It is not a replacement. It is rather making what is considered to be a suitable payment for loss, damage or injury. Africa definitely suffered losses, damages and injuries from the slave trades. These will be discussed in detail in the chapter dealing with arguments in favour of paying compensation. This work however, does not attempt to examine the need for paying reparations for the evils of colonialism.

Genesis of the claims

The first movement towards drawing the World's attention to the evil effects of slavery and the need to pay reparations started in the United States of America. African-Americans started working out an agenda for the payment of reparations in the 1960's. Some of them have since drawn up an invoice and calculated the annual interest.[1] It is not surprising that nearly a quarter of the delegates to the Durban Conference were from the U. S. A., with the majority being African-Americans. Those who attended included some of their leading human rights activists like Rev. Jesse Jackson, Angela Davis and Randal Robinson.

The beginnings of the movement in Africa are rather obscure. The first attempt to formalise the issue and give it a focus seems to have taken place in 1992. In that year, African Heads of states organised a summit meeting at. Dakar, Senegal. At the meeting, the Heads of states appointed a 12 Member Eminent Committee under the chairmanship of the late Chief Moshood Abiola, a prominent businessman and politician to examine the issue and submit their report to the Organisation of African Unity (O.A.U.). The committee's work was to relate to slavery, colonialism and neo-colonialism.[2]

---

1. WEST AFRICA, 17th –23rd Sept 2001, p. 14
2. WEST AFRICA, 24th – 30th July 2000, p. 21

The role of Chief M. K. O. Abiola

Chief Abiola became committed to the cause of reparations. He approached his work with enthusiasm bordering on passion. In April 1993, he organised a conference on reparations at Abuja, Nigeria. Members of the Eminent Committee attended the meeting. It has been reported that chief Abiola financed the conference from his own resources.[3]

Chief Abiola was convinced that Africa stood no chance of achieving her aim, unless he gave the issue the widest publicity and canvassed worldwide support. He started by canvassing the support of the African and African-American community. It is significant to note that a lot of achievements Africa has made at the Global level have always been with the active support, and at times, participation of the Black Americans.

The late chief Abiola did not only prepare the grounds for making claims for monetary compensation, but was also interested in African countries fighting for the restoration of her valuable artefacts which were taken away during the colonial period. He was also convinced that there was the need for African leaders to institute measures that would attract foreign tourists to the many tourist sites spread over the continent. His objective was that, Africa should use this to attract the much-needed foreign exchange into the continent, to be used in alleviating the abject poverty and underdevelopment one encounters all over the continent.

The attitude and role of African leaders

From the start, African leaders have generally adopted a lackadaisical attitude towards the reparations issue that they themselves officially initiated at the Dakar Summit Meeting. As an Organisation, it failed to finance the committee it created. Abiola was left to finance the committee from his own resources.

---

3. WEST AFRICA, 27th Aug - 2nd Sept 2001, p.

There was only one African Head of state who gave Abiola and the committee financial support. That was a former Nigerian head of state, General Ibrahim Babangida.[4]

Up to the time the World Conference against racism, racial discrimination, xenophobia and related intolerance was held at Durban, South Africa form August 31st to September 8th 2001, African Heads of states and the O.A.U. had not done the amount of work that assures positive results. The issue of reparations for slavery and colonialism was billed to be discussed and a decision taken. The whole world was there, despite the official boycott by the U.S.A. and Israel. The U.N.O. was represented. Many N.G.O's were there. More than 10,000 people from different ethnic and cultural backgrounds from every part of the world were present. Before the conference, African Heads of states and other political leaders had been raising a few uncoordinated voices here and there regarding the need for reparations. One of them was Theo-Ben Gurirab, Namibia's foreign minister, who was quoted by "Anti Slavery" in the "reporter" of October 2001, as having said, "A majority of us believe that the past of the slave trade can only be settled in two stages: firstly through an apology, which is an affirmation of one's humanity; and secondly, through reparations".[5] Certainly some African leaders made efforts to carry the world with them to obtain some form of reparations for these two evils. But, their efforts were simply not enough, especially when one finds oneself pitched in battle against the likes of the U.S.A. and Great Britain.

It is however gratifying to note that there was an acknowledgement by the World Conference that "slavery and the slave trade are a crime against humanity and should always have been so, especially the Trans-Atlantic Slave Trade, and are among the major sources and manifestations of racism, racial discrimination, xenophobia and related intolerance".[6]

4. WEST AFRICA 24th – 30th July 2000 p. 21
5. anti – slavery "reporter", Oct 2001, p. 5

6. *anti-slavery* "reporter", Oct 2001, p. 4

The attitude and role of Nigeria

Nigeria is one African country that has taken the reparations issue seriously. The role of the late chief Moshood Abiola of Nigeria has been mentioned. The role and attitude of a former Nigerian head of state General Ibrahim Babangida has been mentioned. Under her current president, General Olusegun Obasanjo, the country launched its first Black Heritage festival towards the end of May 2001.[7] The festival aimed at showing its drama, dance, music and slave trade history to an international audience. The festival was held at Badagary, which was one of the leading ports for exporting slaves outside Nigeria in the Trans-Atlantic Slave Trade era. To climax the festival, the organisers arranged a re-enactment of the process involved in the Trans-Atlantic Slave Trade. It included the capture of the slaves and their transportation to the coast to be loaded aboard the ships that carried them across the Atlantic to the New World. Those who attended the launching included Nigerians, African-Americans resident in Nigeria and fifty visiting American mayors.

The organisers made sure that some aspects of the festival had a direct bearing on the reparations issue. These are the dramatisation and venue chosen. They were meant to transport the viewers back into history, to enable them become direct observers of the trade as it was taking place. This could not but stir their hearts and conscience against the inhumanities of the trade, and win them over to the side of the reparationists.

The issues involved in reparations.

The proponents of reparations are agreed on the need to pay compensations. Beyond that, they give different reasons why compensations should be paid, the form the compensation should take, and who the beneficiaries should be.

The O. A. U. directed the Eminent Committee it set up in 1992, to focus attention on slavery, colonialism and neo-colonialism.

7 *Daily Graphic*, 29th May

The late chief Abiola, the chairman of the Eminent Committee, was interested in paying monetary compensation to Africa as well as returning all the artefacts taken away by Europeans to Europe during the colonial period.

Professor Ali A. Mazrui, a member of the Eminent Committee is reported by West Africa Magazine No. 4236 of 24th – 30th July 2000 as having stated that they were looking at "... a different form of reparation... transfer of resources, or a Marshall Plan for Africa, though the one we know was for reconstruction for war-torn Europe. We could talk of reparation in the form of power sharing – increasing Africa's representation on the institutions of the World Bank and the I. M. F. in spite of the fact that Africa has not yet got the resources to support such increase in representation".[8] Some of the views of Professor Mazrui are rather interesting. He is of the view that Africans suffered martyrdom. He added that the perpetrators must be made to feel guilty and they must also be made to pay accordingly. In his words as reported by West Africa No. 4236, "...getting Africans to take the cause of reparations for enslavement serious is itself an uphill struggle. So we don't take our own martyrdom as a people seriously enough. This is where we can learn from the Jews. They suffered and they used their suffering as a basis for solidarity, as a basis for making sure other people feel guilty for making them suffer. They have received millions from the Germans for the Holocaust."[9]

Some Africans are advocating the transfer of skills as part of reparations. They are of the view that the centuries of the slave trade destroyed the skills of Africa. Many people with all forms of skills were exported. The business of capturing and selling slaves over three centuries distracted the attention of Africans from the exercise of their technological skills. At the same time, they were pushed to the position of being mere recipients of finished European goods. Thus, by the time the slave trade was abolished Africa had experienced a skills development deficiency of over three centuries and had acquired a dependency syndrome.

8/9 Quotes in WEST AFRICA 24TH – 30TH July 2000, p. 21

A panellist on the Ghana Television programme dubbed TALKING POINT raised other dimensions of this argument in October 2001.The Radio Gold program of Ghana called "Konkonsa Reporting" discussed the same issue the day after the TV program. The panellist postulated that America is deliberately encouraging the current brain drain from Africa. The topic under discussion was BRAIN DRAIN. He said America was doing so through clever schemes such as the American Lottery. He added that the American government should be made to pay compensation to the Ghana government for this. His stand was that the amount to be paid should be equal to the amount spent on training every one of the professionals who leave Ghana to work in America. Although the discussion focused on Ghana, his arguments can be extended to cover the whole of Africa. The Radio presenter, the following day, virtually repeated the panellist's arguments as if they were his original ideas. What he added with emphasis was that the American government owed Ghana, and, as such the latter should submit the bill to the American government for payment.

Germany has also mentioned some of the grounds for which Africa should be paid compensation. "Anti Slavery" in its "reporter" of October 2001 carried a statement credited to Joschka Fischer, the minister of foreign affairs of the Federal Republic of Germany to the effect that "past injustice cannot be undone. But to recognise guilt, assume responsibility and face up to historical obligations may at least give back to the victims and their descendants the dignity of which they have been robbed." From this, it is clear that the main reason why Africa should be compensated is because she was robbed of her dignity.

The renowned British human rights organisation, Anti-Slavery International, which was founded in 1839 and is the world's oldest human rights organisation, has shown keen interest in the issue of reparations for slave trade victims. It advocates the payment of compensation. It is of the view that genuine reparations should be made by those who benefited from slavery to slave trade victims. The organisation further considers that, there should be "accurate documentation as well as material compensation." The compensation should "redress slavery's impact whenever it still has perceptible effects on the most disadvantaged groups and communities."[10]

The view of the United Nations Organisation, as expressed through its sub-commission on the Promotion and Protection of Human Rights is worth noting. Its view was crystallized in a resolution it adopted a month prior to the conference on Racism, Xenophobia and related Intolerance held in South Africa. The relevant part of the resolution stated that countries, which reduced other peoples to slavery as well as colonising other people, have a "historic responsibility" and the responsibility "should be the subject of solemn and formal recognition and reparation."[11]

At the close of the World Conference on Racism, the compromise text adopted by the more than 160 countries that participated recognised slavery as a crime against humanity and offered a package of economic assistance to Africa.

10/11. anti-slavery "reporter" Oct. 2001, p. 4

CHAPTER 5 | Arguments in favour of paying reparations.

The slave trades undoubtedly had a lot of evil effects on Africa and the Africans within and outside the continent. It is for these reasons that some Africans at home and abroad and some white human rights activists are making demands for the payment of compensation for the victims.

One commonly cited effect is the reduction of the population of the continent. The exact number of people lost to Africa may not be known. With regards to the Trans-Saharan slave trade, the lowest figure quoted by historians for those believed to have landed safely in the New World is 10 million. One historian has stated, " It is possible that about twenty million West Africans were taken away to the New World--."[1] Some very recent evidence suggests that between 1500 and 1890, about 22 million slaves were exported from the whole of black Africa to all parts of the world.[2] Many slaves of the Atlantic system died in transit. They could not survive the dehumanising conditions they were subjected to. Some died from hunger, diseases, suffocation and suicide. Others were deliberately thrown overboard to drown on the high seas for misconduct, or while the ships were being chased by the British Naval Squadrons for transporting slaves during the abolition era. About two million slaves are believed to have died in transit between Africa and the New World.[3] Many Africans also lost their lives during the numerous inter-ethnic wars fought for the purpose of capturing slaves and also during the numerous slave-raiding activities. Some also died while being marched from the interior to the coast, and even in the dungeons of the forts and castles and in the slave cages while awaiting embarkation to the New World. Lives were also lost during the Trans-Saharan slave trade. The deaths were associated with slave wars and slave raids. But the largest numbers died while being

1. F. K. Buah, 1979, p. 64
2. B. A. Ogot (ed), 1992, p. 83

3. K. Sillington, 1989, p. 174

transported across the Sahara desert. They died mainly from hunger, dehydration, exhaustion and at times getting lost in the desert or being overwhelmed by the sandstorms of the desert. East Africa also lost many souls through wars, raids and transportation to the coast and across the Indian Ocean.

Another bad effect of the slave trades in general and the Atlantic Slave Trade in particular is the increase in inter-ethnic wars. One very important contributory factor to this was the introduction of guns and gunpowder. Actually, when Europeans first landed in Africa, they were reluctant to sell guns to Africans because they were convinced that it would be tantamount to providing Africans with knives to cut the throats of the Europeans.[4] From the second half of the 17th century, they changed their minds and started supplying Africans with large quantities of guns and gunpowder to facilitate the capture of slaves. African communities turned against each other with the deadly weapons. Some of the wars fought from the inception of the slave trade and the introduction of guns and gunpowder had the sole motivation of securing slaves for export. Many African societies abandoned their former traditional practice of exhausting every possible peaceful means of settling misunderstandings between them and embarking on wars only as the last resort. They started fighting upon the slightest pretext. The point has been made that Europeans supplied the guns to induce the natives to fight each other in order to generate captives for sale. Europeans must therefore accept responsibility for these wars as well as the carnage and destruction of property associated with the wars.

At times, some of the Europeans did everything to undermine the authority of some African rulers as well as destroying their kingdoms where the policies of these rulers worked against the desire of the European merchants to acquire slaves for export. A classical example is the role played by the Portuguese in the kingdom of the Congo in the 15th century. The kings of Congo, the Mani-Kongo chose the path of modernisation along European lines. A mani-kongo accepted christianity and western education.

4. J. K. Fynn, R. Addo-Fening, 1991, p.

He wanted to construct modern style or European style buildings with adequate ventilation and roofing facilities such as shingles for example. He wanted to build schools and churches. He therefore welcomed Portuguese architects and mechanics into his kingdom to undertake these social and technological developments. Portugal as a kingdom however undermined his authority by manipulating his sub-chiefs against him, resulting in confusion and the collapse of the kingdom.[5]

Scholars of African history are in total agreement that the slave trades, particularly the Atlantic Slave Trade, has brought about the decline in productivity in almost all sectors of the African economy. One of the reasons is that the active labour force made up of the young and able-bodied was taken away leaving behind mostly the old weak and disabled ones. The slavers favoured people between fifteen and thirty years. They also wanted more boys than girls. Usually they wanted their cargo to consist of about 2/3 boys and 1/3 girls.[6] The basis of most of the African economies at the time was agriculture. Today, it still forms the basis. Under the circumstances, the kind of population left behind could not cultivate and maintain large farms. They could not efficiently maintain even the small farms they made. What worsened the situation was the disincentive to farm. Some slave raiders deliberately destroyed crops on the farms, which, in some cases, had reached advanced stages of maturity. The farm owners got disheartened and did not have the enthusiasm to make new farms or seek to improve their farming skills. It has been suggested that there were some cases of famine in the slave trade era, which had nothing to do with natural causes.

Since it was the same kind of people exported who constituted the suitable labour force for mining and craft industries, there was decline in the productivity of the industries as well. These included gold mining and smithing, pottery, soap making, leatherworks, bead making and cloth weaving. It is argued that, if the growth of the local industries had not been interrupted, they

5. J. C. Anene and G. Brown (eds), 1966, p. 107
6. A. A Boahen with F. A. Ajayi and M. Tidy, 1986

would most probably have advanced to such a high standard that Africa would certainly have been exporting top quality manufactured goods outside the continent to earn the much needed foreign exchange. Africa would most probably not have been depending on the export of primary products, thereby earning minimal foreign exchange. The slave trade resulted in the collapse of some local industries. This happened when Europeans brought foreign substitutes for virtually every industrial product in Africa. European textiles displaced local cloths. European alcoholic drinks displaced the local brews. European leather products, such as footwear, bags, belts, killed the local leather industries. European brass and copper bowls displaced African pottery products. Imported iron stifled the thriving iron industry that was practised all over Africa. European lanterns replaced traditional lamps in most places. One reason for this is that some of the European nations had entered the period of the Industrial Revolution while Africa had not. The manufacturing of European goods with machines made them cheaper and in some cases more attractive looking. Local goods could not compete with them. This development has persisted till today with Africans importing expensive foreign goods while they continue to export cheap unprocessed commodities. It is a sad story indeed for Africa, when it is recalled that shortly after the arrival of the Portuguese in Africa, they for a brief period, exported some African textiles to Europe. "In the sixteenth century, the Portuguese had exported cotton clothes from West Africa for sale in Europe, but in the seventeenth and eighteenth centuries, the trend was reversed".[7] When they arrived, they observed that there were some settled farming communities who wore cotton cloth dyed with indigo. The Portuguese observed that members of these communities also decorated themselves with gold and ivory ornaments. H.W. Jones remarked that "It is one of the harsh and unpalatable facts of history that the principal – almost the only industry of Tropical Africa for many centuries was the trade in slaves carried on mainly by Christian people of Western Europe and Muslim Arabs…"[8].

7. J. K. Fynn, R. Addo – Fening, 1991, p. 214
8. J. C. Anene and G. Brown (eds), 1966 p.

Another misfortune of the Atlantic Slave Trade is that it delayed the development of the cash crops industry in Africa. Some of the Europeans did not want the natives to engage in anything that would distract their attention from capturing slaves for export. A Ghanaian historian, Professor Adu Boahen, has recorded the action taken by the British Board of Trade in ordering Thomas Melvil, their governor at Cape Coast, in Ghana, to stop the Fante from cultivating cotton. The reason they gave was "The introduction of culture and industry amongst Negroes is contrary to the known established policy of this country, there is no saying where this might stop... it might extend to tobacco, sugar and every other commodity which we now take from the colonies; and thereby the Africans who now support themselves by wars, would become planters and their slaves be employed in the culture of these articles in Africa, which they are employed in, in America".[9] The poverty level in Africa today is very high. If Europeans deliberately delayed cash crop cultivation in Africa, thereby denying them an appreciable income from the export of more legitimate commodities, then it is only fair and proper that some form of compensation is paid to ameliorate the poverty and suffering of Africans.

In all the Slave Trades, the foreigners bought the slaves for a ridiculously low price. In the words of one historian, "Slave Trade was an economic exploitation – an unequal exchange".[10] Some facts from the Exploration Diaries of H.M. Stanley, a British-American explorer, which have been quoted by William Kimber and Kevin Shillington, give an indication of how ludicrously low the price at which some slaves sold in some parts of Africa were. Hamed bin Mohammed, better known as Tippu Tip, the greatest supplier of slaves to the East African coast throughout the slave trade period was alleged to have remarked that "slaves cost nothing... they only required to be gathered". His people sold "12 or 15 slaves for 35 pounds (16 kilos) of ivory". The same source reports that "A sheep is said to purchase

9. *Quote in* A. Boahen, 1966, p. 113
10. J. F. Ade Ajayi and I. Espie (eds) 1965, P. 249

43

one [tusk of] ivory, 12 slaves purchase an ivory. In Ujiji 12 slaves purchase an ivory"[11]

It should also be noted that, all the European goods exchanged for slaves were expendable. The desirable effect of some of them such as the alcoholic drinks and tobacco was felt for only a few minutes or hours. On the contrary, the human beings exchanged for these commodities were used as means of production. The owners benefited from their services for so many years. Some of the benefits outlasted the lives of the slaves and even their masters.

Both Britain and the United States of America made promise of paying some form of compensation in connection with the slave trade and slavery, which they have not honoured. In the case of Britain, it had to do with abolishing. In 1837, she installed Pepple as king of Bonny. King Pepple was a favourite of the British but was regarded by his subjects as a stooge. Britain signed four (4) Treaties with the king promising "compensation to Bonney in return for the abolition of the slave trade".[12] Britain did not ratify the Treaties. Neither did she pay any compensation. Interestingly, Britain reinstated him in 1854 when she could not get any willing replacement stooge. To be fair to Britain, she did not promise to pay compensation to the natives for taking part in the slave trade. She rather indicated a willingness to pay some compensation if the natives would give up the trade.

The case of the United States of America is different. The American government actually made a promise to the freed slaves, following their emancipation, that each of them would be given forty acres of land and a mule to enable them start life on their own.[13] Abraham Lincoln, the President at the time, issued the Emancipation proclamation on 1st January 1863. All slaves in the confederacy were

11. K. Shillington, 1989, p. 255
12. J. B. Webster, A. A. Boahen, H. O. Idowu, p. 84
13. D. Cameron In WEST AFRICA, 27th Aug – 2nd Sept 2001, p. 21

given legal freedom by the Emancipation proclamation. Practically, not a single black was set free, as the Act affected only the areas under confederate control. The 13th Amendment, which followed, and came into force on 18th December 1865, prohibited slavery in the whole of the United States. The President himself admitted in the Emancipation proclamation that the freedom granted the slaves was a military expediency aimed at helping the Union win the Civil War. Slaves in Southern States, which declared their loyalty for the Union Government, were not emancipated.[14] The emancipation was aimed at encouraging slaves to escape from their masters in the rebellious states of the south. It was expected that the slaves would cross the frontier into the Northern States where freedom awaited them. The American government was not concerned with the welfare and interest of the slaves. Rather, it was concerned with the interests of the nation; the survival of the Union. The emancipation was aimed at getting more recruits into the Union army. The proclamation permitted the recruitment of Blacks into the Union Navy and Army. Conversely, the proclamation aimed at reducing the size and strength of the southern army. Many of the whites in the south had left their homes and businesses to fight in the confederate Army. Their slaves kept much of their businesses going during their absence. Since the Emancipation Proclamation made many of the slaves of the South to escape to the North, some of the masters had no option other than to stop fighting and return to their estates. By the end of the war, 200,000 blacks, who were former slaves had ended up serving in various capacities in the Union Army and Navy, thereby helping to attain Union Victory and keeping the U.S.A. intact as one United Country. Successive American governments may have forgotten the promise to give every emancipated slave 40 acres of land and a mule but the promise nevertheless still stands. Circumstances have changed and the land and the mule may not be the suitable compensation under the changing circumstances of today but can be converted. After all, Great America keeps her promises and she also honours her heroes! The blacks were heroes in as much as they helped maintain the U.S.A. intact as one country.

14. World Book Inc. World Bk. Encyclopaedia, B. Vol, 2 1992, p. 391-2

A view expressed by some of the reparationists is that African chiefs and leaders acted out of ignorance. They had no idea of the tasks the people they sold were going to perform and the dehumanising conditions they were going to be subjected to.[15] If they had known, they would most probably not have sold them.

Some Africans attribute the increasing impoverishment in Africa today to the slave trade. Out of the world's 25 poorest countries, two-thirds of them are from Black Africa. It must be remembered that the Trade lasted for over three hundred years. For all these periods, the young and able-bodied, the active population needed to undertake all forms of productive economic activities such as farming, mining and manufacturing were exported. Since it was much easier and more profitable to capture slaves for sale, the strong and powerful communities and states devoted more time to the trade to the neglect of the productive sector. Weaker communities tended to concentrate on survival strategies, including migrations and temporary settlement patterns, rather than permanent settlement and productive culture. By the time of abolishing and suppression in the nineteenth century, Africa had undergone a cultural change regarding subsistence and production practices. Many communities were not even willing to stop the trade because they could not see an alternative means of survival. In practical terms most African households cannot afford two good meals per day. Their diet is from cheap carbohydrate sources. They are heavily dependent on cassava, maize, guinea corn and millet for example. Many people take their meals with little or no fish or meat. Whatever little fish or meat that is added to the soup or stew is normally for the male head of the family. The wife and children may have very little or nothing. With regards to shelter, decent housing structures are located mainly in the administrative capital towns such as the National capitals, Regional and District Capitals where the affluent of the society live. Even in these settlements it is mainly the foreign nationals, especially Europeans Lebanese and Syrians, native government officials and natives in commerce and industry who live in the decent housing units. The majority of residents who are mainly

15. *C. Duodu in* WEST AFRICA, 27th Aug – 2nd Sept 2001 p. 22

unemployed youth and workers receiving very poor wages live in slums and ghettos. As for remote rural areas, some people live in wattle and daub structures. Some people live in tent-like structures whose walls and roofing are made from fronds of the palm or coconut trees. It is also a common practice to see many people in all the cities and big towns of Africa living off the streets. Many of them sleep in the open in front of shops. They are lucky to have a full night's sleep during the dry season. In the rainy season, they have to get up in the night whenever it starts raining and scuttle for any spots that would save them from getting drenched. As for the politicians, they constitute a privileged class, which has simply stepped into the shoes of the colonial masters, who they mobilized the masses to overthrow.

The poverty level in many countries has reached such a level that, the ordinary folk, who are in the majority simply do not call at hospitals and other health posts when they are taken ill because they know they cannot afford to pay for consultation and medication. They just walk into the chemist's shops and buy drugs off the counter. In many of the countries, hawkers of drugs patrol the markets and streets or display the drugs on tables at vantage points so that the sick persons may buy, or, a concerned relative or friend may buy some for the sick person at home. Another popular alternative is traditional herbal preparations, which are hawked all over. One needs not know the dosage. The sick person may take any quantity, any time, depending upon the seriousness of his ailment. But thanks be to God that in most cases the patients recover at least at the time. Whether there are some later negative after effects, it is only God who knows.

A very bad effect of this abject poverty is that, some of the few doctors, nurses and other para-medical personnel, who have been trained at the tax-payers' expense are leaving the African countries for the rich advanced countries because of a lot of frustrations such as poor salaries, lack of equipment to put their skills to work and lack of facilities for further improvement of their skills and competencies.

To some people, the beginnings of this impoverishment are traceable to the slave trade. Since some whites are said to be the initiators and perpetrators of the slave trade, which started the impoverishment process, then they must accept responsibility for the current socio-economic woes of the Africans. To them, it is only fair and proper that, the whites pay some form of compensation to Africa to be utilized in turning around the fortunes of the present and future generations of Africa.

As already briefly mentioned, some reparationists argue that Europeans initiated the reprehensible enterprise. When they arrived on the continent, they initially asked for the legitimate natural resources of the continent such as gold and ivory. The natives obliged by supplying these commodities in exchange for European goods. When it suited the Europeans, they asked for slaves and Africans only responded by supplying them with their new demands. This view seems to present the Europeans as playing the active part with the helpless Africans only dancing to the music provided by whites. Consequently, now that it has been accepted by all that it was an evil trade, the whites must accept responsibility for the tune they played which they caused the natives to dance to.

Furthermore, attention is also drawn to the fact that in some instances, African kings were coerced into meeting the demands of some of the white men for slaves. Of all the European countries, Portugal was the guiltiest party. The activities were centred in the regions of Angola and the Congo. The Portuguese slaving activities in Angola were direct and aggressive. They imposed taxes on the chiefs of the region. The taxes were to be paid mainly in slaves. They introduced some measures to facilitate their trading activities between the coast and the interior, which produced the effect of impressing upon the native rulers Portuguese power and might. This intimidated them to do the will of the Portuguese. They built forts in the hinterland as centres of their military strength to protect their slave caravans. These forts frightened any local chief who might be tempted into opposing the Portuguese in any way. The chiefs also saw the half-caste Portuguese called pombeiros, ruthlessly ravaging their territory acquiring slaves. This frightened them into engaging in local wars, or organising raids to secure captives to pay the taxes imposed on them by the Portuguese. In addition, the Portuguese were prepared to go to any length to undermine the authority of any chief in the territory whose activities in any way tended to frustrate their goal of securing the maximum number of slaves. They actually undermined the authority of the king of the Congo, the Mani-Kongo, among his sub-chiefs and collapsed the kingdom, because of his opposition to the slave trade. The Mani-kongo had chosen the path of development by accepting Western education, Portuguese teachers, Christianity and Christian missionaries, Portuguese architects, mechanics etc. This choice was however at variance with the interests of Portuguese traders and the Portuguese state at the time. The Mani-Kongo's choice had to bow to the interest and the power and might of the traders, to the extent that the kingdom collapsed.[16] Within the period, Luanda became the leading slave port of the African continent.

Some reparationists also draw attention to the fact that some Africans were uprooted permanently from their homeland into alien lands. The slaves, especially the first generations were placed in a very tragic situation, which was full of permanent lamentations. Even later generations of slaves who were born in their new countries constantly questioned why and how fate had dealt with them so cruelly. The despondency of the uprooted Blacks in the U.S.A was forever recorded for posterity in what became known as Negro Spirituals. One of the most moving ones was Psalm 137, which they adopted;

1. *By the rivers of Babylon, there we sat down, yea, we wept, when we remembered Zion.*
2. *We hanged our harps upon the willows in the midst thereof*
3. *For there they that carried us away captive required of us a song: and they that wasted us required of us mirth saying, sing us one of the songs of Zion*
4. *How shall we sing the LORD'S song in a strange land?*

Many Black Americans have emerged as leaders of civil and political rights movements. All of them have had large following. No matter how one looks at it, the plight and experiences of the

16 J. C. Anene and G. Brown, 1966,

leaders and their followers were rooted in the fact of their uprootment from their native lands and implantation in new lands with different culture and values. There was the World of the whites and the world of the Blacks co-existing in America. Until recently, many Blacks in the U.S.A were confused. It was clear to them that they were living in their own distinct World while the whites were living in another distinct world. The whites had drawn a line between them. The world of the blacks was harsh and full of many disabilities and restrictions. They did not like their world. They wanted to escape from it. Escape meant either a forward movement; a penetration into the White world or a backward movement, a movement into Africa, their homeland and the world of the Blacks. Black leaders with different perceptions and convictions started emerging and started attracting followership to make some movement.

Booker T. Washington was the first Black American activist to rise to fame in America. His perception and conviction was that the Black American should uplift himself onto a higher pedestal in America by striving to acquire agricultural and manual skills. Washington's doctrines were embodied in what became known as the Atlanta Compromise. The Atlanta compromise in effect accepted racial discrimination. What the Black-American had to do was to work at self-actualisation. His convictions moved him to take the practical step of establishing a technical school at Tuskegee to provide Black Americans with the relevant knowledge and skills for their advancement.

The next Black American who rose to prominence after Booker T. Washington's death was William Dubois. He was a great opponent of Washington. His view was that since Blacks had been uprooted from Africa and resettled in America, the latter had become their home. What had to be done was that White Americans must be compelled to grant the Blacks' equal rights. For this purpose, he founded the National Association for the Advancement of Coloured People (NAACP) in 1909. He also established the magazine called "Crisis" to articulate his views worldwide. Black Americans have, in the main, sought racial equality and the destruction of the colour bar system through the NAACP.

The Black-American who has advocated one of the most radical and revolutionary methods of solving this peculiar problem, which faced them, was Marcus Garvey of Jamaica. He formed the Universal Negro Improvement Association (UNIA). He was passionately anti-white. He was ultra-Black. Garvey "preached racial purity, upheld a black Christ and black Madonna and called upon his followers to forget the White gods." His slogans were "Africa for Africans", "black redemption not as humble beggars but as proud soldiers demanding and forcing concessions; equality in America, freedom in Africa, dignity everywhere; a share in the World economy and a black Christ overseeing all".[17]

What made the Black Americans look forward to "penetrating" America or backwards to returning to Africa was not solely because they had been uprooted from their homeland into an alien land. Perhaps, more importantly was the fact that they were deprived of all their human rights. They were slaves pure and simple! Before emancipation, their ancestors had been properties of their masters. The plantation slaves worked from dawn to dusk. On the fields, the whips in the hands of their supervisors were their dread. While most of them would not end their own lives, natural death would be a most welcome visitor.

Another reason why some Africans, Black-Americans and even some Whites are asking for reparations is that the labour and other forms of contributions of slaves and slave descendants have contributed tremendously to the development of parts of the New World especially the USA. There is the feeling that it is now the turn of the USA and other countries, which benefited from slave labour to reciprocate by paying compensation that, will help in the development or progress of Africans and Black Americans.

Although the USA is the most developed and the most powerful state in the World today, her beginnings were very simple. The basis of her economy at the time the states were being founded was agriculture in the South and mining in the North especially

17. J. B. Webster and A. A. Boahen with H. O. Idowu, 1967, pp. 298- 300

The North East. The Southern states were engaged in the cultivation of king cotton. There was also the cultivation of some tea, tobacco and sugar cane. Black Slaves were used to do all the manual work, starting from the clearing of land through planting and harvesting. In the Northern States black slaves were used on a lesser scale with some white slaves and white labourers to mine the gold silver and other minerals. Agriculture and mining produced the wealth of the nation. The cultivation of tobacco for example made Virginia the wealthiest British colony in the New World. America, Britain, France, Portugal, Spain and other European nations benefited directly and indirectly from Black slave labour, which they used to develop their countries. Reparationists are convinced that these beneficiaries of slave labour should reciprocate by paying compensation to help improve upon the lot of the victims of slavery; even though the present generation of Africans and Black-Americans are many generations apart from the direct victims of slavery.

Again, slaves and their descendants contributed to the increase in population of the countries to which they were exported. By 1790,the total population of the U.S.A was about 3,929,214. Out of this, Africans numbered 759,208. In 1765, the Africans population actually outnumbered the White population in South Carolina. The European population was 40,000 while the black population was 90,000.[18] Many of the blacks were put to productive work on farms, in mines and in white homes.

Today, the U.S.A has a National network of railway lines. She even boasts of two trans-Continental lines between the Eastern and Western coasts. The development of the network started on a modest scale. At the early stages, cheap slave labour was used to clear pathways through forests and grasslands for the lines to be laid. Slave labour was again used to carry and lay the lines. Slave labour was also used to construct motorable roads and bridges.

Many of the early public buildings belonging to the states and the union also made extensive use of Black slave labour in

18. J. K. Fynn and R. Addo-Fening, 1991, p. 212

performing those tasks, which did not entail any specialised skills.

Blacks in the Diaspora have made many political contributions to their new countries. As usual, the U.S.A is the leading country. Perhaps the greatest political contribution that Black-Americans have made to their new country is that they helped save the country from disintegration during the civil war. Both the positive and negative roles they played helped turn the tide in favour of the Union forces. Their enlistment into the Union Army increased its numerical strength by 200,000. They fought valiantly, both in the army and the navy. One of them was Robert Smalls. He defected to the North with a confederate ship called the Planter and handed it over to the Union. He himself became a member of the union Navy. Many of them laid down their lives to help keep America united. About 40,000 Blacks died fighting during the Civil war. The majority fought for the Union. They fought valiantly. The topmost Military Award of Honour was given to twenty-three (23) blacks for distinguishing themselves in the Union Forces.[19] The negative contributions included desertion from their southern masters and outright defections. Some of those who remained in their master's estates were not exactly loyal to their masters.

Black Americans made tremendous contributions to the American war effort during World War I and World War II. More than 360,000 of them served in the U. S. A. Armed Forces during World War I. They were formed into all-Black Units and many of them served with excellence. In World War II nearly 1,000,000 of them served in various capacities in the U. S. A. Armed Forces. They have since served in every external war that the U. S. A. has fought, including Vietnam and the American led military campaigns in Afghanistan.

Reparationists contend that if Blacks contributed in saving America from disintegration, and helped her through one of the most critical periods of her history, now that she has grown to

19. The World Book Encyclopaedia, B. Vol, 2, 1992, p. 392

become the most powerful and prosperous state in the world, it is incumbent on her to reciprocate by paying some form of compensation to Africans and Black-Americans, many of whom are wallowing in poverty.

Blacks have also made contributions to the politics and governance of the U. S. A. and some European countries. In America, some have risen to become members of the president's cabinet. The first of them was Robert C. Weaver. He served as the Secretary of the Department of Housing and Urban Development.[20] Andrew Young, who was born in 1932 and is still living, is a Black-American who served as the United States Ambassador to the U. N. from 1977-1979. He did much credit to the U. S. A. on the international scene by contributing immensely towards the attainment of majority rule in Africa, especially South Africa. Before then, he had served as Mayor of Atlanta, and Congressman from 1972 until 1977 when President Jimmy Carter gave him the U. N. appointment. An astute Black American diplomat called Ralph J. Bunche brought honour to the U. S. A. when he won the Nobel Peace Prize in 1950. He was the first black person that ever won the prize. Thurgood Marshall was appointed to the U. S. Supreme Court in 1967. He was the first Black-American to rise to that position in the Judiciary. Shirley Chisholm was elected to the House of Representatives in 1969, being the first black woman to do so. She, and others like her have made positive contributions towards the enactment of legislations in the U. S. A.

America is also noted for her achievements in the field of Sports. Many of the people who have made the achievements for her are Black-Americans. In 1936, Jesse Owens became the first person to win four gold medals at the Olympic games. This feat, which took place in Berlin, compelled Adolph Hitler to leave the stadium to avoid congratulating him, for being a non-Aryan and a Black for that matter.[21]

Today, boxing is one of the most popular sporting activities,

20. J. K. Fynn and R. Addo-Fening, 1991, p. 212
21. Grandreams-Ltd. The Concise Encyclopaedia 1996, p. 455

especially the heavyweight rank. Most of the World tournaments take place in the U. S. A. especially Las Vegas. Many of the leading names in boxing are Black-Americans. The person who has made boxing the popular game it is today is Mohammed Ali, a Black-American who was called Cassius Clay – until he converted to Islam. He was born in 1942 and is still living. Ali was the world's heavyweight champion from 1964-67, 1974-78, and 1978. Tall and handsome, he will always be remembered by his epigram, "I'll fly like a butterfly and sting like a bee". Another famous Black-American heavyweight boxer is Mike Tyson. He is a household name regardless of his shortcomings and he has brought a lot of honour to the U.S.A.

The reasons why Blacks at home and those in the Diaspora (due to slavery) need to be compensated are obviously numerous. Central to these are the exploitation of Africa, dehumanising slaves and their descendants and deriving tremendous benefits from slaves and their descendants.

CHAPTER 6 ||| Compensation for Helpless Victims

There is no doubt that a group of people has legitimate claims for compensation. It is the true and helpless victims of the slave trade and slavery. The direct victims are dead and gone. Their descendants are spread all over the world, with the greatest concentration in the Americas and the Caribbean islands. Others are in Europe, Asia, and the islands of the Indian Ocean. Some have remained distinctively African in terms of ethnicity. Many others have become mixed races through inter-marriages. This last group is no longer easily identifiable.

One of the reasons why they are entitled to compensation is that they were forcefully and permanently removed from their societies and transported into alien lands. Their ancestors were not goods to be collected from their source and transported elsewhere. They were human beings with rights; to live in their native lands. In many African communities up till today, there is veneration of some objects to the extent that they may not be moved from their locations or they may not be touched let alone destroyed without the performance of special customary rights. A typical example is the royal stool, which serves as the symbol of office of many chiefs. They are considered to be sacred. It is a taboo for even the chief to sit on this sacred stool. It is a taboo for the ordinary person to step into a sacred grove, let alone cut or fell a tree in the grove. The groves are venerated because some of them serve as burial places for the royalty or because they accommodate the community shrine. Violating these taboos call for special pacification rites, which in the past included the culprit being sacrificed to the gods. There is no doubt that every human being is of greater value than these objects, and the spirits behind them. The abused human beings are more worthy of compensation than the gods, ancestral spirits and all other forms of lesser spirits that attract so much veneration from the Africans. We are living in an age of respect for human rights and reconciliation. Even though the generation of Africans directly sold and bought is gone, it is proper and fitting to compensate their living descendants wherever they are today. It is also necessary to compensate them for planting their ancestors and for that matter the present generation forcefully and permanently in alien lands. Many of her first generation of slaves died prematurely by agonising over their predicaments in their new and alien environments. They could not overcome the constant consciousness that they had forever been cut off from loved ones.

Up till today, there are some Blacks who are unable to identify themselves completely with their new countries; even rich and powerful America. They still feel nostalgic about Africa and would like to relocate but find it impracticable. But a few Black-Americans have been returning. Some have started returning to Ghana for example, especially after the country started organising the PANAFEST.

There is the need to pay some compensation to the millions of slave descendants all over the world, whether they have returned or decided to remain in their new homes. Perhaps compensation will serve as a sort of palliative to set their souls at rest.

Blacks of slave origin in the Diaspora, especially in America are entitled to compensation for the loss of human rights and untold human suffering they and their ancestors were subjected to. Before the passing of a lot of anti-slavery and anti-racist laws in the U.S.A., they had no civil rights whatsoever. Up to the 1860s, they were subjected to serious abuses in many of the states.[1] Within the period, Blacks and a few White humanitarians fought for improvements in the treatment given to Blacks. Their modest successes attracted repression from some White reactionaries. Many racist legislations were passed. They were the so called "black codes," of 1865 and 1866. Some of the codes denied Blacks education in some states. They were denied freedom of movement, especially from one town to another, unless the person carried a special pass. Blacks could not meet with their friends unless they had the permission of their masters. They could be arrested in some states for being unemployed. Some codes debarred Blacks from owning lands, while some imposed night curfews on them. These are only a few of the disabilities

1. World Book, Inc. B. Vol. 2, 1992, pp.391-3

suffered by the Black-Americans under the "black-codes". It is not all White Americans who were anti-Black or racists at the time. Some of them vehemently opposed the discrimination and maltreatment of the Blacks by their fellow Whitemen. The discrimination was most pronounced in the Southern States. The White human rights activists were mostly from the Northern States and also members of the Republican Party. Those of them who were Congressmen were tagged Radical Republican. They pioneered the enactment of legislations, which granted equality of blacks with whites in some areas. Congress passed the Civil Rights Act of 1866, which accorded Blacks the rights and privileges enjoyed by full citizens. The 14th Amendment of 1868 gave full guarantee of citizenship to Blacks. Some Southern Whites could simply not bear the "abomination" that was being perpetrated by the humanitarians and the Union government. Even before the passing of the 14th Amendment, White racists from the South had murdered about 5,000 Blacks in the two years covering 1865 and 1866. The hatred was so intense that the murderers found it expedient to carry out some of their dastardly acts in schools and even in churches! Rather than witness Blacks breathing air of freedom on the streets of America or in American public houses such as schools and restaurants, some white Americans were prepared to form murder organisations such as the Ku Klux Klan. Behind their racist hoods, they were prepared to murder not only Blacks, but also fellow Whites who sympathised with the Blacks and were prepared to champion their cause. It is a tribute to the USA, that, as a nation, its heart remained loving and caring and it had the resolve to give protection to the Blacks, and deal with the racists by passing the Ku Klux Klan Acts (the enforcement Acts). The enforcement Acts empowered Federal troops to use force to implement the voting rights of Blacks. The second half of the 19th century witnessed a lot of vicissitudes on the Black human rights scene. Perhaps a critical factor was the conviction carried by many Southern Whites that the Black was inferior to the White in all positive aspects. This included intelligence, talents and moral standards. Based on this assumption, some Whites could simply not accept the fact of equality with Blacks despite Federal laws granting equality. In 1881, Tennessee passed a law providing for racial separation on passenger trains. In 1890, Mississippi introduced measures aimed at excluding Blacks from exercising their right to vote. Some of the voting requirements for Blacks were the need to pass some reading and writing tests, and evidence that they had paid the poll tax. This was at a time when the majority of Blacks did not have access to education and were therefore illiterate. In addition, most of them did not have any viable employment and therefore had no regular income to enable them pay the poll tax.

In 1883, the US Supreme court actually declared the Civil Rights Act of 1875 unconstitutional. The 1875 Act granted Blacks the right to be admitted to all public places. In 1896, an interesting development took place in the Constitutional history of the USA. There was a Supreme Court ruling which came out with a "Separate but equal doctrine". What the doctrine involved was that there could be segregation but the public facilities available to Blacks should be equal to those of Whites. For example, there could be White schools and Black schools provided the schools were equal. This could work only in theory but not in practice. Thus, the 1896 ruling virtually invalidated the Civil Rights Act of 1866 and the 14th Amendment to the Constitution.

In the Southern States, the early 1900s witnessed a reversal of almost all the political gains made by Blacks in America. By 1907, almost all public facilities in the South were subjected to racial discrimination. These included schools, buses, trains, restaurants and even churches. By 1910, Blacks in almost all the Southern States no longer had the right to vote. Laws were enacted aimed at excluding Blacks in the Southern States from engaging in a lot of economic activities. They could not own saloons for example nor teach. The idea was to push them into the very low jobs including pushing them into becoming tenant farmers or sharecroppers.

It became necessary for Black-Americans to intensify their efforts at liberation by forming civil rights movements in the 1900s. Malcolm X (1925-65) was one of the leaders of the movements. The sense of loss of human rights moved him and others of his thinking to react by forming a movement for the unification of black people all over the world. The movement they formed in

1964 was called the Organisation of Afro-American Unity (OAAU). It is not all his fellow Black activists who approved of his beliefs and methods, and in 1965, he was killed. Three people were jailed for killing him. Two of them were fellow Black-Muslims.

Another famous Black-American leader was Martin Luther King Jr. (1929-1968). He led the fight for equality and justice for Blacks and all races in the U.S.A. Like Mahatma Ghandi, he advocated and used peaceful means for the attainment of his objective. He preached "non-violent resistance". In 1964, he was awarded the Nobel peace prize for his leading American Blacks to use peaceful means only in the fight for social, economic and political equality in the U.S.A. Ironically, he died a victim of violence. James Earl Ray, a Whiteman who had escaped from jail, shot him to death on April 4, 1968 in Memphis. It could not be established whether he acted alone or with some accomplices. In his days, Black passengers in Montgomery and many other Southern cities could sit only on the back seats of public buses. He organised a Black boycott of the buses in 1955. The boycott proved successful and they were permitted to sit anywhere they liked in the buses. Martin Luther King Jr. organised many peaceful mass demonstrations for the liberation of his fellow Black-Americans from inequalities and injustices. They had no voting rights and consequently no say in the government of the U.S.A. One of the memorable mass demonstrations was the march of over 200,000 people from the Washington Monument to the Lincoln Memorial. It was on that occasion that he made the famous utterance "I have a dream that one day this nation will rise up and live up to the true meaning of its creed. 'We hold these truths to be self-evident; that all men are created equal.'"

The numerous civil rights activities that were taking place within the period moved the American Congress to enact the Civil Rights Act of 1964. In 1965, the Voting Rights Act was passed. These legislations helped move the Blacks towards their goal of equality and justice. The fight was tortuous and at times bloody. Even today full equality has not been achieved practically. The situation is however much better.

All said and done, using the standards set by World morality today, it is only fair and proper that these identifiable and true victims of slave trade and slavery be given some form of compensation. Similar identifiable victims in other parts of the world need to be compensated

CHAPTER 7 | No Compensation for Africa

One of the reasons given by reparationists for demanding compensation for Africa is that Europeans and some other foreigners forcefully removed Africans form their societies into alien lands and rendered them rootless. The current developments taking place in Africa, especially in West Africa, where most of the slaves of the Atlantic system were exported, do not make this a valid point for the payment of compensation. Many Africans of both sexes, and of all ages are wilfully struggling to leave the continent for Europe, the Americas and Asian countries. Today, African migrants scattered across the world is about 50 million.[1] The majority of them are illegal immigrants. They are mostly unskilled labourers seeking any kind of work to do. Some of them end up in detentions in foreign countries, or end up in slavery conditions, living in the same conditions and doing the same jobs that emancipated slaves in America resisted over many years, for which reason they formed the civil rights movements and got America to pass the Civil Rights Acts.

Many of them want to leave Africa for good. They spend fortunes to acquire passports and visas through legal and illegal means. Many of them use various kinds of illegal means and routes in their attempts to reach their foreign destinations. Some make hazardous journeys across the Sahara desert. They arrange to be smuggled in boats from Morocco to Spain. Some of them perish in the desert. Some also die while trying to cross the Mediterranean Sea. On 30th May 2001, 15 Africans were reported missing in the deep seas while making an illegal crossing from Morocco to Spain. They were in an over crowded boat. The boat was intercepted by a Spanish Civil guard patrol. The illegal passengers panicked. They caused the boat to capsize.[2] Such attempts have become the rule rather than the exception and this has compelled the Spanish Coast Guards to intensify their patrol of the sea separating their Southern Coastline from

1. I. S. Diop in WEST AFRICA, 30th Oct – 5th Nov. 2000, p. 23
2. *DAILY GRAPHIC*, June 2, 2001, p. 5

Morocco. The DAILY GRAPHIC of July17, 2001 reported that about 15,000 African immigrants tried to enter Spain illegally and scores drowned in the attempt. Some of the bodies of those who drown are at times found washed ashore Spanish beaches. On 15th July 2001 for example, the Spanish police found six such bodies on their beaches. They also arrested one hundred and thirty illegal immigrants.[3] The dead and the arrested were voluntarily fleeing Africa. All such people always know what they are fleeing from. They always have high expectations for their future in the "Promised Lands". But, they cannot tell for certain what awaits them. All the same, they are prepared for anything outside Africa - including slaving it out. They are even prepared to die trying. Their conviction is that, there is after all nothing to lose, but everything to gain.

Some Africans also try to stowaway in merchant ships berthed in their harbours. The Daily Graphic of Ghana for example, reported in its issue of June 2, 2001 that there was a crackdown on stowaways by security forces. It added that the phenomenon was becoming a nuisance on ships bound for Europe and the Americas. Those caught aboard the ship had been hiding for three days before their discovery. Those caught were made up of three Camerounians and seven Ghanaians. The ship, which was loading at Takoradi harbour, was an Italian vessel. There are about fifty million African migrants outside the continent. Some are students. Some are highly educated, qualified and skilled personnel. Of the qualified and skilled personnel, some get dignified and well-paid jobs. However, some of them do not get the sort of employment they trained for. They end up doing menial jobs and at times living in slavery conditions, with the hope that someday, they would get the right kind of work. Even this group of people prefer to live and work in Europe and America and other foreign countries rather than return to Africa for even the top-level public service employment. As for the overwhelming majority of the 50 million who have no professional qualifications or skills, they only rely on chance to secure any kind of employment. They take up such kinds of jobs

3. *DAILY GRAPHIC*, July 17, 2001, p. 5

that they would not do in Africa; cleaners, petrol station attendants, poultry farm attendants and farm labourers just to mention a few. African critics considered an observation made by Bryan Edwards most insulting. He stated that African slaves were "removed to a situation infinitely more desirable even in their native Africa".[4] The African mind rejects this. However, the activities of some Africans, especially the unskilled and the under privileged class give some credence to this view. He added that slaves in Africa in the years before and during the period of the Atlantic slave trade could not look forward to security either of their property or their person. The fact is that many freeborn commoners in Africa today, have no property and are also unlikely to acquire any in their lifetime in Africa. Indeed, a renowned Ghanaian pastor of the International Central Gospel Church, Rev. Dr Mensah Otabil, came close to corroborating Edwards' observation in one of his programs on RADIO GOLD on October 29, 2001. He said that many Ghanaians were still flocking to America. He added that the Ghanaians considered the bombs of Osama bin Laden to be safer than the poverty of Africa. He postulated that, if three ships should dock along the Ghanaian Coast, and an invitation should be thrown to Ghanaians to embark without visas, you would see pastors rushing to embark in competition with members of their congregation. He added humorously that the pastors would have suitable Bible quotations to support their action, such as "If the Lord opens the floodgates..."

These developments call for African governments and reparationists to sit up and try to find solutions to this adventure into slavery and the unknown rather than insisting on being paid compensation for the Atlantic Slave trade. If there is any compensation to be paid, it must go to the true victims, the living descendants of those who were forcefully and permanently uprooted.

One interesting argument advanced by Africans in their demand for compensation is that the slave trade and slavery was forced

---

4 J.C. Anene and G. Brown, 1996, p.92

upon them. Available historical evidence is to the contrary. Slavery was practised in Africa before the Whiteman ever set foot on the continent. Likewise, it was independently practised in Europe, Asia and all other parts of the world. Even in Biblical times, slavery was practised. The African partners in the Atlantic Slave trade voluntarily and happily entered into partnership with the external slavers. There were only a few dissenting native voices. King Pepple was a ruler of Bonny in the present day Republic of Nigeria. He defended slavery at the time the British were trying to suppress it. According to him, " ... slavery was ordained by God and sanctioned by the juju priests."[5] Many African kings used slave labour on their plantations. King Gelele of Dahomey for example used war prisoners on his royal farms.[6] When the slave trade was abolished, some of the European countries, led by Britain encouraged the development of the legitimate trade in Africa. Some African kings responded by establishing large-scale farms. They however started using slave labour, similar to how it was practised in the New World.[7]

Many prominent Africans today are beginning to question whether the trans-Atlantic slave trade was an entirely European affair, or whether Africans were willing partakers. President Abdoulaye Wade of Senegal has made the admission that his ancestors had a ten thousand-man army out of which two thirds were slaves.[8] Many other states conscripted slaves into their armies.

Before the arrival of the Europeans, there were some cases of war captives and criminals being donated to some gods in some parts of Africa. An example is the "Trokosi" practice, which still exists in some parts of Ghana. Female children and close relations of criminals were donated to the "Trokosi" shrine. They became the property of the shrine for the rest of their lives. The victims lost their rights and did the bidding of the gods or their custodians. In some parts of Africa, there was always the possibility of having

5/6. J. B. Webster, A. A. Boahen, H. O. Idowu, 1967, p. 73
7. J. B. Wester, A. A. Boahen, H. O. Idowu, 1967, p. 83
8. *Special Report.* WEST AFRICA, 27th Aug – 2nd Sept 2001 p.19

such slaves sacrificed to the gods if and when the need arose. Anene and Brown have further remarked that in the pre-Atlantic slave trade, "captives of war from other groups could be sold, could be sacrificed and could be eaten."[9] The annual incursions of Dahomey into Yorubaland were partly for the purpose of securing slaves to be sacrificed to their gods. Many of the slaves of Benin in Nigeria were used for human sacrifice. This earned Benin the name "City of Blood".[10]

Again, Africans reduced some of their slaves to eunuchs in order to assign them some special roles in society. The leading task for them was reliable harem keepers. Some were also made courtiers and palace guards. The practice was widespread in North and West Africa. Almost all the states of the West African Sudan and the West African coast engaged in the practice. Examples are Ghana, Mali, Songhai, Asante and Benin. The castration of the African by the African was one of the ingenuities of the traditional elite to safeguard some of their peculiar interests.

Many slaves in Africa were used as beasts of burden. They served as head porters for the goods of their merchant masters from one market centre to another to be bartered. There is a fast resurgence of this form of slavery in another form in some African cities like Accra and Kumasi. The difference is that the victims have no permanent owners and they also receive paltry fees for carrying their temporary masters' and mistresses' loads from one point to another fixed destination in the city centres. In Ghana, the female head porters are called "Kayaye" whilst their male counterparts are called "Kayayo". Some may be as young as ten years and the overwhelming majority are teenagers. Being homeless and extremely poor, they are vulnerable to many abuses including forced sex. Thus, many of them are found with fatherless babies tied to their backs while performing their daily exactions.

9. J. C. Anene, and, G. Brown (eds), 1966, p. 94
10. J. C. Anene and G. Brown (eds), 1966, p. 107

Many well to do homes, by African standards had domestic slaves. Some of them were actually bought for the purpose. Others were people who were pawned for debts owed by family members. Some victims pawned themselves to people they owed. The treatment given to these people by their masters and mistresses depended upon the nature and disposition of the masters and mistresses.

Some Africans teamed up with Portugal to practise an intra-African slave trade to their mutual benefit before the trade was transformed into the Atlantic Slave trade.[11] In 1497, Shama in Ghana bought slaves brought in by the Portuguese from 'Rio de Esclavos' (Benin in Nigeria). In 1505 and 1535 the Portuguese sold some other African slaves to Elmina in Ghana. The Ghanaians used them in mining gold, picking kola nuts and as domestic slaves. One thing, which is certain, is that, besides the victims, all the other parties were prepared to play their roles for personal gain. The sources were prepared to supply, the end users were prepared to buy and the Portuguese were prepared to be slavers.

African rulers and other leaders were happy to supply European merchants with slaves for the material benefits they obtained. One of the most cherished materials was textiles; for the man and his wives. The dignity and social status derived from the use of the gaudy fabrics meant much more to them than the disposal of human beings, who, in most cases were not related to him or did not come from his community. If a community member was involved, he was most likely a criminal or some other form of undesirable person. Even more important was the European gun and gunpowder. It was not forced on the African. It was something he craved; an object of power and might and a symbol of manhood. It did not take any whiteman to convince the African of this. He formed his own opinion, and took his own decision. The European alcoholic drinks were also very desirable and continue to be so up till today. After all, it brought merriment to the individual and the whole gathering within a few

11. J. K. Fynn and R. Addo-Fening 1991, p. 208

minutes of its administration. It was handy and did not easily go bad like the local brews. One could reach out for it anytime of the day or night and experience an abrupt transformation, an exhilaration. It was not clear whether it was more suitable for festive occasions or mournful occasions. Then, there were other goods, looking glasses, and treated tobacco with the accompanying smoking pipes. There was local tobacco, but of course the whiteman's was more desirable. There were the beads. The women liked the beads. The men liked the women; not one, not two. After all, Africa was a polygamous continent. The more gifts of beads, earrings, etc. that the man could give out to the women, the more women he could get. The woman, no, the women, would also make it worth his while. Of course, the Europeans would exchange their goods only with slaves and so the Africans had to strive for as many slaves as possible. After all, most of the African suppliers had the mentality of Tippu Tipp who said that "slaves cost nothing ... they only required to be gathered." Tippu Tipp was not a pure African. He was of mixed Nyamwezi, Arab and Swahili origin. He was one of the leading slave traders of his time, but he and the pure African slave traders had the same mentality.

There were some other very important needs of the Africans. He did not have to be told by any Whiteman what his needs were. Ostentatious funerals. They were vitally important. They still are. A Danish chaplain on the Ghanaian coast in the early eighteenth century, Johann Rask, reported, "men were not averse to selling their wives and children or relatives in order to defray the cost of ostentatious funerals."[12] The Yao who occupied the East and southeast of Lake Malawi also sold their fellow Yao into slavery to the French in the closing decades of the eighteenth century when they could not get enough captives from other ethnic groups. The "prazeros" of lower Zambezi sold their own subjects, and even at times, their own chikunda armies.[13] Tippu Tipp was right. He gathered from outside but others went further by gathering from their communities and their families. The

12. J. K. Fynn and R. Addo-Fening, 1991, p. 213
13. K. Shillington, 1989, p. 251-2

whites have abolished the Atlantic slave trade. They have however not abolished ostentatious funerals. Strange things continue to be done to sustain the funerals, which have become far more ostentatious today than they were at Rask's time. But that is beyond the scope of this work. Even so, it will be interesting finding out whether the implications of ostentatious funerals today give Africans a moral stand to demand compensation for slavery and the slave trade.

African leaders wanted European goods so much, so that, some of them started making the sale of their subjects into slavery the only punishment for all crimes. A man in the region of the Gambia River for example was sold to European slavers for stealing a tobacco pipe.[14]

Another group of Africans who voluntarily played a vital role in the Atlantic slave trade system for personal gain were the "landlords", also referred to as "protectors".[15] They rented out lands to Europeans along the coast for the construction of suitable structures for assembling and warehousing slaves before they were exported. The structures took the form of forts and castles, trading posts, baracoons and pens. They received payment in the form of customary dues and at times a commission on each slave sold. The trade was a golden opportunity for the African landlords to make good money without sweating.

A few voices have been raised to the effect that Africans did not know how the slaves they sold were going to be used. It is asserted that if they had known the inhumane conditions they were going to be subjected to, they would not have sold them. This stand is rather sad. The fact of the sale itself was immoral and criminal. If it suited them to effect the sale, then they naturally should have known that the buyers, the bona fide owners of the property were free to use the slaves anyhow they wished. Considering the fact that in Africa at the time, some slave owners did sacrifice some to the gods, and did eat some of

14. J. B. Webster, A. A. Boahen, H. O. Idowu, 1967, p. 75
15. J. F. Ajayi and I. Espie, 1965, p. 250

them, then it is difficult to accept the argument that the same Africans would not have sold slaves to Europeans and other foreign buyers if they had known that they were going to use them as farm and mine labourers and domestic slaves. As has been mentioned elsewhere, some of the slaves were made to perform the same tasks in Africa.

Historians and reparationists, especially African historians and reparationists have sought to put all the blame for the slave trade on Europeans for introducing guns and gunpowder. It is true that the introduction of guns and gunpowder seems to be the single most important factor for the increase in the volume of captives in Africa. All the same, the argument is rather puerile. It is an insult to the intelligence of the Africans at the time and even now. The trade was an economic transaction involving offer and acceptance on the part of both the European buyers and the African sellers. All the parties independently considered the issues and implications involved in the transaction. Each side made use of its intelligence at the consideration stage and then took a decision. Granted that the Africans and the Europeans had equal intelligence, then it would be improper for the African to blame the white for his choosing to accept the white man's guns in exchange for slaves. The African view will be accepted and pity extended to him only when he makes an admission that the Whiteman used his superior intelligence to influence him to accept guns for slaves.

Another interesting point raised by some reparationists is that the slave trade was an un-equal transaction. Europeans cheated Africans by exchanging fanciful and transient goods for a means of production. In other words, the slaves were sold too cheaply. As such, it is only right that the descendants of the buyers should pay some form of compensation to the descendants of the sellers. It is not clear whether those who hold this view have a way of computing the objective difference in price between the slaves and the goods exchanged for them. It is also not clear whether they want the difference to be paid - perhaps with interest! Will it ever be possible to place a realistic monetary value on each of the slaves sold or even a single one of them? Supposing this was possible, would any transaction in this direction not be tantamount to consummating an unfinished business? Are reparationists prepared to identify themselves with this development; that Africa be paid the balance due her before the chapter on the Atlantic slave trade is closed?

A lot can be said for and against the view that the Atlantic slave trade, or the slave trades are responsible for the low productivity in Africa today, or over the years. The common reasons given are that the young and able bodied were taken away, i.e., the productive labour force, and the old and weak were left behind. Additionally, the European goods exchanged for slaves served as a disincentive for the development and growth of local industries. First of all, labour alone is not all that is needed to increase productivity. The other factors of production are equally very important. Besides, labour, if it is untrained and undeveloped, could be a serious liability for most sectors of production. Even in modern agriculture, untrained labour is of little use. There is evidence that the so-called productive labour force exported to the U.S.A. for example had to be given various forms of training by their masters before they could perform appreciably as planters, harvesters or even as domestic slaves.[16] In terms of development, the Southern States, which had greater numbers of slaves, lagged behind the Northern States, which had fewer slaves. After the civil war, and the Consolidation of the Union, purposeful policies were initiated and implemented by successive American governments to bring up the South by way of development. Supposing the productive labour force were exported during the slave trade era, many generations of young and able-bodied have been born since abolition. There has since been years of opportunity for generations of young and able-bodied Africans to increase productivity, if that is all it takes. This has however not happened. Or would those who hold this view like to say that the old and weak who were left behind continued to reproduce weak people?. In any case, one must not forget that there was never a time when all the young and able-bodied people were taken away from any part of Africa. Similarly, it is high time that Africans stopped blaming today's

16. M. G. Kelty, 1937, 43

undeveloped local industries on the European goods introduced in the years of the slave trade. Manufacturers of goods will always look for markets for their products. Even within Africa, localities that have had an urge over others by way of industrialisation have always exported their products to the disadvantaged areas. Rather than wasting time fighting for compensation for the mistakes of engaging in the wrong economic relationships with the advanced Western nations in the past, it will do Africa a lot of good if she realised that the time spent complaining simply means time granted the advanced countries to continue widening the gap by way of development. How Africa solves this problem is an African problem and she has to awake to reality. The chorus by African leaders for an even playing field is sentimental. The fact is that there is never an even playing field in the economic relationships between countries. Even within one country like the USA, there is never an even or level playing field between the competing economic industrial and commercial enterprises. The causes of Africa's low productivity today lie far beyond these arguments. If the right answers are to be found and positive steps taken towards increasing productivity, then Africans must let go these arguments and grow out of the past.

One of the adverse effects of the slave trades on Africa is the reduction in population. It is not certain whether this is being made an issue for reparations. If it is, what should be noted is that, if the population of Africa had been much greater than it is today, there is a high probability that the continent's problems would have been worse. The writer is not happy at the loss of our brothers and sisters forced into the Diaspora as a result of the slave trade. The sad fact is that most of them would have been wallowing in abject poverty today, had they remained in Africa.

Many Africans resisted the abolition of the slave trade. If they had their way, the trade should have continued indefinitely. The attitude and actions of our ancestors do not give us the moral justification for making claims for compensation against whites for a trade that whites particularly Britain had to bribe and coerce our ancestors to stop. King Kosoko of Lagos for example had to be deposed in 1851 by the British because of his unwillingness to stop the trade.[17] Lagos under Kosoko was a strong base for the trade.

There are some abominable customary practices that are comparable to slavery and the slave trade, which Europeans tried unsuccessfully to get Africans to give. They did not succeed until their exit upon the attainment of independence by African countries. These include human sacrifice and ritual murder.

One of the key reasons why reparationists are convinced Africa is entitled to compensation is that Holocaust victims have been paid some reparations.[18] While the two experiences share some things in common, there are some major differences, which set them apart. Holocaust is the word used for the near deliberate elimination of Jews in Europe by Nazi Germany under Adolf Hitler, following his assumption of office in 1933. When Germany was defeated in World War II, Jewish survivors of the Holocaust demanded reparations. With the support of the civilised nations of the world, they have been receiving payments from foreign states and banks over the years. The new Germany that emerged in 1949, (the Federal Republic of Germany,) accepted to pay over 700 million dollars to the State of Israel for her persecution of Jews in Europe. The United States of America has led a search for Jewish Holocaust assets hidden in various sources. News, com. au reported that "Heirs of Holocaust victims have received 10 million US dollars from a massive search of Swiss bank accounts dormant since World War II..." The payments made were in response to some of the claims submitted by surviving relatives of Jews who had deposited monies in Swiss accounts, and were later killed by the Nazis. Norway set up an official committee on 29 March 1996 "to investigate the fate of Jewish property in Norway during and after World War II." Based on the Committee's recommendations, the Ministry of Justice drafted a White Paper that was adopted by all political parties in Parliament on March 11, 1999 agreeing to the payment of reparations. The reparations involved two things: an official

17. F. K. Buah, 1979, p.114
18. D.Cameron in WEST AFRICA, 27th Aug – 2nd Sept 2001, p. 21

apology to Norwegian Jewry and cash compensation of about Nok 450 million (70 million dollars). The cash compensation was to be made up of individual compensation and collective compensation. Prior to this Norway had been paying a complex form of compensation to their Holocaust victims.[19]

The deliberate persecution of the Jews itself started in the years leading to World War II and continued with intensity up to the very end of the War. It also started within the limits of Germany and continued to experience territorial expansion with Germany's conquest and control of more European countries. It was motivated by Hitler's pathological hatred of Jews, to the extent that he ended up killing about two thirds of the Jewish population numbering more than six million. He spread the net of death to cover some other populations like Poles, Slavs, Gypsies, Jehovah Witnesses, Communists, and homosexuals.

The process started in Germany by first of all defining who a Jew was. The Nazis then started the actual attack by carrying out economic persecutions. Right from 1933, Jews working in public employment were dismissed. Measures were instituted to deprive Jewish professionals like doctors and lawyers of their clients. There was a liquidation of Jewish firms. Under the policy of "Aryanization", Jewish businessmen were forced to sell their businesses to Germans at ridiculously low prices. Since the motive was to deny Jews any means of livelihood, all Jews working in the liquidated or sold businesses were sacked. To further impoverish them, the proceeds accruing from the sale of their businesses were heavily taxed. The State also taxed whatever savings they had.

The second form of persecution of non-Aryans, particularly Jews, took the form of the subjection of their persons to various forms of torture and even death, especially during the war years. In Poland, which was occupied by Germany in 1939, the Germans started by confining the Jews in ghettos. The ghettos were fenced with walls and barbed wire to prevent any escape. The inmates

19. Anti-Semitism Research. Fall 1999, Vol.111. No.1

74

were poorly fed usually on grains and vegetables such as carrots, beets and turnips. Germany invaded the USSR and the killing of Jews started very early there. In 1941, the German SS let loose 3000 of their members in the occupied territories to kill Jews on the spot. Many Jews were shot to death in ravines and ditches mainly at the outskirts of towns and cities. Nazi hatred for Jews continued to grow to the extent that in 1941, Herman Goring, the second in command in Germany directed the Chief of the Reich Security main office, Reinhard Hedrich to organise the "Final Solution". This involved deportations to ghettos and the setting up of Death camps. The camps had many ingenious facilities and schemes for killing people. These included shooting, starving and gassing. There were facilities for incinerating people after killing them to minimise the chances of the outside world getting to know what was happening in the death camps. Some of the inmates were subjected to all forms of medical experiments including sterilisation. Those who faced the earliest killings were the very old men and women and very young boys and girls. Members of the middle age group who had no relevant vocational skills were also subjected to early death. This is because they could not be put to work to produce anything for the State. The strong and able-bodied, who had skills needed to produce items needed by the States were allowed to continue living for as long as they were fit and productive and well-behaved. If their services were no longer needed or they were suspected of treachery their lives were terminated. Jews were hauled from all over occupied Europe to the death camps. They came from Norway, France, Germany, Italy, Hungary, Czechoslovakia, Poland, Greece and Yugoslavia. The largest death camp was at Auschwitz in Poland. Most of the death camps were in Poland. Some other notorious camps were at Sobibor, Treblinka and Kulmhof.[20]

The Holocaust was a peculiar event and does not lend itself to an adequate comparison with the slave trades. It was a deliberate plan to wipe out helpless groups of people, particularly Jews. Unlike the slave trade where Africans sold their own, there was

---

20. Microsoft (R) Encarta. (R) 1998 Encyclopedia

no Jewish complicity in the Holocaust. It is this one significant difference that entitles one group to reparations and disqualifies the other. It is this one difference that places Africa in the group of those who should be paying compensation rather than a recipient.

Indeed, the conscience of the whole world was so aroused by the atrocities of a powerful state against a powerless dispersed ethnic group that most nations of the world supported the creation of a haven for the surviving Jews in Palestine. Thus, Israel was established as a Jewish State in 1948. It is also worth mentioning that some of the reparations being paid to Jews today are savings made by their own forebears in foreign accounts.

The reparations issue is rather selective. Attention for claims is focused only on the rich nations of the West especially the USA, Britain, France, Spain, Portugal, Holland and Denmark. The relatively poor countries of South America and the Caribbean islands, which also benefited from slave trade and slavery, are not being targeted. The Asian States and Indian Ocean islands that benefited from the East and North African slave trades are also not being targeted. There are indications that the considerations that are influencing reparationists are the wealth of the nations coupled with their sensitivity to human rights issues. In terms of wealth, some of the Arab countries are as rich, if not richer than some of the Western European states. They have amassed a lot of wealth from their petroleum industries. Human rights issues are however not exactly at the centre stage of their politics. Reparationists appear to be aware of the fact that claims against them at this stage will appear to be strange to the majority of their citizens and will not stimulate internal pressure upon the governments to pay.

African Perpetuation of Slavery

The greatest indictment against Africa's quest for reparations for slavery and the slave trade is that she is still actively engaging in the malpractice.

Buying and Selling

Buying and selling of human beings still takes place in Africa. The practice is however discreet and covet because various forms of laws, both National and International, prohibit the practice. It has been declared a criminal offence punishable by severe sentences. However, police reports, media reports and reports of many civil organisations, especially Non-governmental Organisations show that the malpractice goes on, on a daily basis.

THE MIRROR of Ghana, in its June 23, 2001 issue reported that one Benjamin Yaw Adu attempted selling his 12 year old nephew to under-cover police agents in the Central Region of the country in the same month for about ¢60 million (8450 US Dollars) but was arrested, and sentenced to thirty months imprisonment. Yaw Adu certainly knew that there were some people engaged in buying human beings. Where he went wrong is that he could not establish contact with genuine buyers but instead fell into the trap of the police. The DAILY GRAPHIC of Ghana, in its July 16, 2001 issue reported that an International ring involved in luring and buying African women and sending them to Europe was alleged to have been busted by the police in Guinea in July 2001. The traffickers were alleged to be mainly Nigerians. They were alleged to be sourcing most of their victims from Nigeria and exporting them to southern Europe, mainly through Spain and Italy.

Although the true volume of the trafficking is not known, it has been estimated that it generates about 10 billion dollars for those involved in Africa.[21] The problem was serious enough to prompt the Economic Community of West African States (ECOWAS) in co-operation with the United Nations Office for Drug Control and Crime Prevention (UNODCCP) and the Centre for International Crime Prevention (CICP), with support from the government of Japan to organise a one week meeting in Accra, Ghana, starting from October 23, 2001 on this and related issues. The experts at

21. WEST AFRICA 30th Oct – 5th Nov. 2000. p. 21

the meeting were to, among other things, formulate a political declaration against trafficking in human beings, and to come out with a plan of action to eradicate trafficking in all member countries. The conference was also to deal with trans-national crimes such as slavery, prostitution and women and child labour. Many interested international and non-governmental organisations attended the meeting. Some of them were UNICEF, ILO, and IOM[22].

Sources and Destinations

Human trafficking in Africa today takes place at three main levels.

First of all, there is the purely internal trafficking. In each country, victims are generally trafficked from the rural settlements. Thus, in Ghana for example victims are trafficked from the poor rural villages to Accra, the national capital, and Kumasi, the second largest city, for example. In Cote d'Ivoire, Togo, and Nigeria, for example, their national capitals of Abidjan, Lome and Lagos are the main destinations from their rural villages. Within the same country, some rural areas at times serve as destinations from other rural settlements. The receiving centres are usually engaged in some economic activities, which require cheap or free labour. The common activities include fishing, small scale illegal mining of gold and diamonds and cash crop farming, especially cocoa cultivation. Some fishing settlements, along the banks of the Volta Lake in Ghana for example attract slave labour. In the case of the Sudan, slaves are usually trafficked from the south, which is under the control of the Sudan Peoples Liberation Army (SPLA) to the North, which is under the control of the National government.[23]

Secondly, there is the trans-border trafficking involving most West African and Central African countries. This trans-border trade does not follow any distinct directional flow. There is a

22. THE GHANAIAN TIMES, Oct.24, 2001,p.3
23. Anti-Slavery Int "reporter" Oct. 2001, p. 5

criss-crossing of boundaries. Some victims are taken from Ghana to Togo, Togo to Ghana, Nigeria to Ghana, Ghana to Nigeria, etc. However, there appears to be greater movement towards the relatively richer states like Gabon, Nigeria and Cote d'Ivoire. These states are oil-producing countries and there is the expectation of traffickers that they can make more money when they deliver their cargo at these centres. In April 2001, the whole World was shocked by the news that the ship, the Etireno was carrying children from Benin to Gabon. There were 43 children aboard. They were mostly from Benin, Togo and Mali. Fortunately, Gabon prevented the ship from docking.

The highest level of the trafficking involves exporting the victims to overseas countries. The favoured destinations are Western Europe and the oil-rich Arab countries of the Middle East. The DAILY GRAPHIC in its July 16, 2001 edition reported that an International ring involved in the luring and buying of African women and sending them to Europe was alleged to have been busted by the police in Guinea. The traffickers were reported to be mainly Nigerians. The victims were said to be 30 would-be prostitutes. The arrested traffickers were reported to be twenty. Indeed Europe is expressing concern at this phenomenon. WEST AFRICA N° 4250 reported the concern raised by the Italian Secretary for Foreign Affairs at Dakar that, "Human beings are not commodities." He pleaded with African countries to co-operate with the "host" countries in working towards the return of the illegal immigrants to Africa to contribute towards the continent's development.[24]

How The Slaves Are Obtained

Some of the slaves are obtained through abductions. Typical areas where this method operates are countries engaged in civil wars, such as Sudan and Liberia. In the Sudan, it is usually the north that abducts victims from the SPLA-controlled south. About one hundred and twenty-two women and men were abducted in Sudan in January 2001. In the countries that are

24. W. Af rica, 30th Oct – 5th Nov, 2000 p. 23

enjoying peace, it is usually very young boys and girls who are abducted because of the obvious security problems of transporting abducted grown-ups to the receiving centres.

Both young and old are lured through deception by the traffickers. The traffickers at times influence young women to travel with them by promising them good jobs with attractive pay, or the opportunity of acquiring advanced vocational skills, which will prepare them for self employment, or securing good jobs at their destinations. These vocations include hairdressing and catering, or even fashion and designing. Similarly, parents of young victims are told their children will be enrolled into good schools or given good vocational training as seamstresses and hairdressers for example. Some are even told that their children would serve as house-helps to some rich women. They are told that the girls would perform light duties with attractive wages. The parents are happy to release their children when they think of the transformation that will take place in their own lives when they start receiving the occasional remittances that would be sent to them as part of the earnings of their children. They are also told that the child would be given some attractive "end of service benefits" either in the form of cash, or some property like sewing machine, or both. Children as young as five years, are at times trafficked. Girls, in their twenties are also trafficked.

Some poor parents in the poverty-stricken rural areas at times deliberately send some of their children to well to do relatives in urban centres to work. This arrangement, it is hoped, will relieve the parents of some of their responsibilities, assure the child of her daily bread, and at the same time bring the parents occasional income for augmenting the family budget. According to a source in African Centre for Human Development, male contractors tend to befriend their victims and lure them away with promises of a better future.

Reasons For The Trade

No matter how one looks at it, the economic forces of demand and supply are at the root of the trade.

There are two aspects to the demand side, i.e. the economic aspects and the social aspects. At all the "host" centres, there are some enterprises looking for cheap labour. Within fishing communities, the boat owners want people who will work for them, if possible without receiving any pay. They find the answer in trafficked young boys. The extent, to which the fisherman can expand his fleet of canoes, depends to a very large extent upon the number of people he can get to man them at little or no cost. In some of the fishing communities along the banks of the Volta lake for example, some fishermen obtain young boys from other parts of Ghana and give them basic training skills in fishing, such as rowing the boats, casting the nets, and mending nets. Some of the boys start their slavery under their masters or owners when they are about five years old. They usually spend the daytime mending nets and depart for fishing in the night. They spend all night fishing. According to some sources, they get around four hours of sleep in twenty-four hours. They are at times fed once a day on scanty and poor quality food. Although they claim they eat in the canoes while fishing, some observers have expressed doubt, as they have not seen any form of food being packed into canoes before setting off. When the nets are entangled by some of the tree stumps and branches in the Volta Lake, these children are coerced into diving to stay under the water for as long as it takes to retrieve the nets. Some of them die in the process through suffocation.

There is demand for cheap labour in many of the cocoa farms in West and Central Africa. Cote d'Ivoire, Gabon and Cameroon are usually centres that attract labourers who work under slavery conditions. The owners of the farms are aware that their labourers are illegal immigrants who have no rights in their host countries. While a few give adequate feeding to the labourers, most are fed on one or two poor meals a day and they are paid slave wages.

Some illegal miners also look for workers to help them mine diamonds and gold. To reduce operational cost and maximise profit, they choose to go in for minors and illegal adult immigrants who cannot claim the protection of the laws of their host countries. They are used to work for long hours, poorly fed and housed and subjected to all manner of insults and punishments.

Some proprietors decide to establish sex businesses in the urban towns. They know that some people want to wind down after the days' frustrations. Others want peculiar ways of celebrating their successes. Some of these entrepreneurs look for all kinds of structures and convert them into brothels. They then recruit prostitutes and engage them under all sorts of "contract agreements". The victims become sex slaves to their masters and mistresses. The master may make use of any of them at anytime without having to pay her anything. The sex slaves who are taken to European countries are subjected to worse treatment. Their passports are confiscated by their patrons, upon arrival. Some of them are required to pay a fixed sum daily to their patrons, allegedly to be used in defraying the cost of their passports, visas transportation from Africa, housing and feeding, etc.,. No matter how much they try, they are never able to realise the stipulated amount. Consequently, they are never able to earn their liberation and they remain sex slaves to their proprietors (proprietresses) and their male clients.

Many people in the urban centres are engaged in the rat-race of making money. They want to operate many businesses at the same time. Some set up local restaurants called "chop bars". Some are in the iced water-selling business. Others are engaged in selling bread, oranges, sugar cane, etc. Whatever the type of business, some of the owners decide to recruit young boys and girls who may work for them at little or no cost. The child may be involved in cooking which includes sweeping the premises, setting the fire, washing the dishes, serving customers and pounding fufu, etc. All the same, she could be given a single scanty meal a day. The lucky ones could get two meals a day. The hawkers are usually given specified amounts of money they are to realise by the end of the day's work. Failure to make the amount could attract beatings or denial of food. Some of the female victims could have pepper or other hot preparations inserted into their private parts. As for sleeping places, a veranda, the chop bar or a wooden kiosk would do. Some things common to all these slaves are the long hours of hard work, scanty and poor meals and the short hours of sleep.

It is now a common practice for urban women to look for housemaids who are now euphemistically referred to as "house-helps". This is a major cause of child trafficking in Africa. This is so because; even the parents of the trafficked child see nothing wrong with the practice. However, in many cases, the trafficked child becomes a slave to her mistress, the mistress' husband and their children. In some instances, she does not eat the same quality and quantity of food with the other members of the household. At times, such a child will have to wait until everybody else finishes eating for her to tidy up the table and wash the plates before she eats. She must eat at an obscure part of the house and sit on the floor while eating. She does the washing of all the clothes. While other members of the household go to school, she is denied this facility. On Sundays, while other members of the household go to church, she must stay behind to play the role of a security guard in the event that some robbers decide to raid the house. At times, her mistress' husband or male children may sexually abuse the house-help. She dares not complain.

Some of the causes of the trafficking and slavery are poverty, greed and ignorance.

There is serious poverty in Africa. The degree of poverty afflicting some of the rural communities, and even some of the unemployed population in the urban and sub-urban communities, cannot be imagined by any of the government officials of African countries responsible for trying to find solutions to the poverty problem. Many rural communities undertake farming as the source of their livelihood. Their farms, in terms of size, may best be described as gardens. The average farmer in many communities considers it a great achievement when he cultivates one or two acres of food-crops for the year. The farmer and his family depend on the produce from the farm to fee themselves and at the same time sell some for income to provide themselves with all their needs throughout the year. Thus, they usually prepare carbohydrate meals from cassava, maize, millet or sorghum with soup or stew consisting of water, pepper, very little or no tomatoes and no fish or meat. Some of these families have a special treat when the farmer is lucky and his trap catches some rodent like rats or grasscutter. Occasionally, the trap catches an antelope or a deer. Many farmers sell the whole catch for some extra money to enable them indulge themselves with some local brew.

These rural families are usually relatively large. The man may have two or three wives with each of them bearing children for him. In most traditional societies women consider it a great blessing when they have many children, even when they have no visible source of income. More and more un-married teenage girls continue to have children with different fathers and a lot of times they never get married to any of them.

Members of these families are not able to buy any decent clothes. They go in for the worst and the cheapest second-hand clothes imported from the western developed countries. Some of them look up to their relations in the urban centres to supply them with these second-hand clothes. They are not able to send their children to school, even when no school fees are charged. They cannot buy the exercise books, the pencils and pens and the school uniform. Their parents want them on the farms and they are also happier on the farms where they might be lucky to roast some tubers for the day's brunch instead of remaining in schools without breakfast and lunch.

The state of abject poverty in which these children wallow dispose them and their parents to accept offers extended to them by the visibly well to do trafficker who lures them with promises of offering them a better future.

The story is no different for the urban or sub-urban poor families. They see signs of good life all around them and they are anxious for a transformation of their circumstances. Both parents and children respond favourably to the overtures made by a trafficker who promises to take a child away to another city or some other location for good development or a promising vocational training.

In many African cities, there are many young unmarried and unemployed women who have to fend for themselves. They want food, clothing and spending money. Some of them voluntarily enter into prostitution and become sex slaves. Some of them are lured by traffickers into sex trade in foreign countries. Some of them are lured into drug trafficking where they end up being virtually enslaved by their employers.

Greed and covetousness influence some parents to push their children into slavery. Some parents, especially women have the love for material possessions. They want more than they have. Some also want to have everything that their friends and other associates have. They decide to use their children especially their daughters to perform any kind of work that will serve as a source of income for the acquisition of property. They end up releasing such children to agents who undertake the placement of their children as domestic slaves, hawkers and vendors, chop bar attendants or even prostitutes.

Another factor that influences parents and guardians to release their children to traffickers is ignorance. Such parents and guardians honestly do not know the fate that awaits their children or wards. They believe the deceptions or the traffickers. When they later get to know, they spare no effort to rescue the victims. Ignorance influences some independent adult females and males to become prey to traffickers. They honestly believe that genuine legitimate and decent jobs await them. When they later discover that they have been deceived, they make every effort to disentangle themselves.

Organised slave trade hinges around the role of the trafficker. He is the critical link between the demand and supply causes for the slave trade. What is the motive of the trafficker? The answer seems to be the desire to catapult himself onto a desired level of the social status in order to enjoy the life style associated with that status. Many people are craving mansions, big and expensive cars, trendy clothes, frequent trips to the cities of Europe and America, good food and drinks and the ability to pick and drop women in the case of men. The key to this is wealth. The trafficker wants the big money for this life. The trafficker realises that he stands no chance of making the big money through conventional means. In some cases, he realises that he cannot get any employment because he has no education, or where he is educated, he has not acquired the relevant knowledge and skills needed by employers, and so he resorts to the illegal means of acquiring wealth where no employer is going to consider academic qualifications. Similarly, there are some educated and qualified people whose services are actually needed by local employers. Unfortunately, some of these people have aspirations similar to those described above. When they consider the pay levels that obtain in their countries, they realise that they stand no chance of getting close to their ambitions on their salaries. Some of them therefore decide to become traffickers. It seems to be axiomatic that the illegal jobs of the world are very lucrative. This applies to human trafficking, and drug trafficking among others.

Blaming Others Syndrome

Shifting blame is a human weakness that is exhibited by all communities all over the world. In Africa, it has been one of the major obstacles to national development. In the era of coup d'états in the 1960s and 1970s civilian regimes and military regimes accused each other of being totally responsible for the woes of their countries. Now that coups are generally out of vogue because of the stance taken by the Western democracies (and embraced by the OAU and its successor the AU), the internal ruling political parties, and the opposition parties continue to shift total blame onto each other for the woes of their countries. Each sees itself as being totally white and the other being totally black. Where there are misunderstandings between neighbouring ethnic communities, there is the tendency for each side to put total blame on the other. The truth however is that no side is usually totally wrong or totally right. The facts of the slave trades show that Africans and foreigners share the blame. Any attempt to shift blame on any group of foreigners will only be a manifestation of the blaming others syndrome. Once Africans share the guilt, there is no justification for demanding any compensation.

CHAPTER 8

Some Extenuating Acts Of Some Of The Accused

The demands for compensation focus on only the negative role played by whites. No cognisance is taken of any positive thing done by the accused either deliberately or accidentally during or after the trade.

The abolition of the trade was a British initiative. There were mixed motives in her fight for abolition. The evils of the trade and the grounds for the claims for reparations are basically moral issues. A moral factor that was critical in the abolition process was repentance, the conviction that the buying and selling of human beings was wrong. The British and many whites were well ahead of Africans in this regard. William Pitt (1759-1806), one of the British Prime Ministers within the period, once stated: "How can we hesitate a moment to abolish this commerce in human flesh which has so long disgraced our country and which our example will contribute to abolish in every corner of the globe?"[1] It is in tune with this spirit that a few great men and women in Britain moved the heart and resources of the Nation against the trade and proceeded to influence other slaving states to join in its abolition.

The campaign was not easy. There was internal opposition. There was external opposition - from France, Spain, Portugal, USA and Brazil. But they did not relent. Through diplomacy, bribery and force, they managed to get these countries to give up the trade at different times under varying circumstances.. Most of the effective work towards abolition was done by Britain and the USA. The stoppage of the trade emanated more from their actions than the role of the African suppliers. The illegal trafficking that some Africans are engaged in today suggests that, if today, the parties that Africans are pressurising to pay compensation

1. J. C. Anene and G. Brown (eds), 1966, p. 103

should decide to ask for a restart of the trade, there shall be favourable response from an appreciable number of Africans.

It is bad that whites made overtures to Africans for the start of the Atlantic slave trade system. All the same, the present and future generations of Africans must appreciate and be thankful for the roles some of them later played. These include the humanitarians and all other abolitionists in Great Britain, the British Parliament, the British Judiciary and the British taxpayers. As discussed earlier the humanitarians aroused national consciousness against the evils of the trade and campaigned for its abolition. The Judiciary declared that, the laws of England did not recognise slavery. Parliament enacted the abolition acts. The taxpayers' money paid for the suppression measures. This included the cost of all the resources of the Anti Slavery Naval Squadron stationed along the West African Coast with the Headquarters at Freetown, Sierra Leone. The British government again spent part of the taxpayers' money in bribing or compensating some states before they agreed to stop the trade. This included Spain and Portugal. Even some African chiefs at times received tokens in the form of alcoholic drinks. To help improve the conditions of liberated slaves and assist them in starting life afresh in a suitable environment, some British individuals, a company and the British government co-operated to resettle willing freed slaves from England, Nova Scotia and Jamaica at Granville Town in 1787. This grew into Sierra Leone. The effort was started by Granville Sharp. Merchant-humanitarians formed the Sierra Leone Company to take up the enterprise since Sharp alone could not sustain it. From 1807, "recaptives", i.e. slaves on their way to the New World, who were freed on the high seas by the British Navy, were resettled in Sierra Leone to join the earlier settlers in starting life afresh. Britain took over the Colony and gave it support to enable it grow into a prosperous country. It is unfortunate what Sierra Leone has become today under its independent governments. But even now, she has not been abandoned by Britain, which is helping in her reconstruction, including helping to set up a modern well-equipped National army.

Another effort was made at giving freed slaves a chance to start life afresh in Africa. This resulted in the foundation of Liberia. It started with the resettlement of eighty-eight people from America in 1820. This first batch were settled on the Sherbro Island which is now located in Sierra Leone. The next group were resettled at Cape Mesurado (later renamed Monrovia) in 1821, because of the numerous problems the first group encountered at Sherbro, including native hostility. Although there were mixed-motives for transporting Blacks from America to start life afresh in Africa, a major, if not the chief reason was humanitarian considerations. The enterprise itself was the combined effort of free Black-Americans, American Colonisation Society, which was formed in 1816 by some white Northern American clergymen and Southern slave owners, and the American government. Indeed, it was the government that supplied transport for the first batch to Africa. The USA has given Liberia a lot of support over the years. Again, it is unfortunate what Liberia has become today under her independent governments.

Britain helped to promote the legitimate trade as a substitute for the slave trade, and as a source of income for Africans in territories under her control. Some other European countries did the same. They encouraged the cultivation of cash crops such as cocoa, coffee, the oil palm trees, cotton and groundnuts for the mutual benefit of both parties. The issue of which party benefited more from the new trade system is outside the scope of this work. Suffice it to say that, if the colonial pact, as the economic arrangements in African countries during the period of colonial rule was termed by France, was unfavourable to African states, they have had around half a century of political independence to work out what best suits them. The reality today is that despite their condemnations of colonial rule, the independent Nations of Africa are rushing to their former colonial masters to help them shape their economies. The need for the Western countries, involvement in operating the economies of independent African countries is so crucial that, the attachment of Anglophone countries to Britain only and Francophone countries to France only for example is no longer being adhered to. Because of the desperate need for help, African countries are today rushing to attract foreign investment under terms described in the days of the struggle for independence as neo-colonialism.

One thing that is often over-looked is that, without the introduction of new crops into Africa by the Europeans during the slave trade period, the hunger and poverty of the continent would have been worse than it is today. Two of the crops, which have become staple food items in many African homes, are maize and cassava (manioc). Europeans introduced these from the New World.[2] They constitute a few of the food items that are common throughout the year. They are also cheap and affordable for the poorly paid African workers. In Ghana, President J. A. Kuffuor has launched a special program called the President's Special Initiative on Cassava. It is expected to provide employment and income to many of the unemployed as well as fetch revenue for the country. Europeans also brought sweet potatoes, groundnuts (peanuts), pineapples, papaws, sugar canes and guava from the New World.[3] Besides groundnuts, the others are mostly luxuries as the rural population and the unemployed and low-income workers of the urban and sub-urban settlements cannot afford to spend money on such commodities. The Europeans also introduced some Asian food crops into the countries where they operated. Two of them also form the staple diet of many communities; these are cocoyam and rice.[4] It must however be noted that some historians are of the view that Africa had an indigenous variety of rice before the introduction of foreign ones. Some other Asian food crops they introduced are coconuts, garden eggs and onions. They also introduced oranges, lemons and melons from Europe. Whatever the motives for the introduction of these crops were, they have become a blessing to the continent.

The Europeans introduced western education in their spheres of influence, which transformed into their colonies as a consequence of the partition of Africa. The efforts at promoting western education and Christianity declined during the years of the slave

2/3. J. K. Fynn and R. Addo-Fening, 1991, p. 217
4. J. K. Fynn and R. Addo-Fening, 1991, p. 217

trade. However, the efforts were intensified in the abolition era and after. Many African scholars have tended to criticise the impact of western education on African culture. It is ironical that while the illiterates of Africa are generally the wretched of the continent, those who have benefited from western education are comparatively better off in terms of employment opportunities and sustainable income. The top level of the educated, including those who have specialised in African traditions and culture in the universities tend to move to the developed countries of the West for good employment that guarantees them adequate income, security and comfort. There is general agreement that the world is moving towards globalisation and that Africa cannot afford to be left behind. The bitter truth is that everything that enhances Africa's chances of being a comfortable member of the global world is derived from Western culture, Western languages, technologies, work ethics, and democracy, etc. Everything that keeps Africa on the other side of the gulf is illiteracy and African culture. This theme is again outside the scope of this work, but Africans must be prepared to give credit where it is due.

The western nations who were mostly involved in the trans-Atlantic slave trade are now leading the world in coming out with various conventions guaranteeing the Rights of various vulnerable groups such as the "disabled", the "child" and "women". Many of these disadvantaged and vulnerable groups are in Africa and other third world countries. The whites mobilise human, material and financial resources from their countries to deal with these problems to make life a little bit meaningful to the peoples of these lands.

Many of the European countries, which were involved in the slave trade, also became colonial masters of African countries. There were so many evils of colonial rule and African nations fought hard for political independence. It is however significant to note that even where the fight was bitter and violent, the need to maintain ties with their former colonial masters has been felt. The ties of friendship are voluntary. The rapprochement has been working to the advantage of the African nations as they continue to receive all kinds of support from the former colonial masters.

These include loans, aids, grants, debt cancellations, technical support and various forms of training schemes. Africans have been relying on the Western developed countries to assist them in solving all major internal problems and cross-border conflicts. An interesting development could take place if the reparations issue is pushed too far. The so-called guilty external nations could be presented with the bill for their sins. They could decide to pay and then stop offering any kind of assistance to Africa. Can Africa survive when this happens?

CHAPTER 9 ||| What Needs To Be Done

Identification Of Perpetrators And True Victims

The issue of the Atlantic slave trade has attracted the attention and concern of the whole world. The world did so when it made it one of the topics listed for discussion at its World Conference Against Racism held in Durban, South Africa. It has been postulated within the relevant pages of this work that any examination of the African slave trade for the purpose of any form of remedy should embrace the trans-Saharan and the East African slave trades and the purely internal slavery as well.

One of the first things that the whole world needs to do is to come to a common agreement on who the perpetrators were.

The first obvious group is the suppliers of the slaves. They were the African states and kingdoms of East and Central Africa, West Africa (the states of the Forest Zone and the Sudan), and those of Northern Africa. These are made up of Egypt and the Maghrebian states. The states of Southern Africa were also involved. The whole of Africa was involved either as captors, suppliers or users.

The second group were the external slavers. One sub-group was the Arab and Asian states of the Near and Far East. Almost all of them were involved in buying and selling or making use of slave labour. Some of the leading nations were Arabia, Persia and India.

The next group were the leading European nations at the time, which established commercial contact with Africa. They were Portugal, Spain, Holland, Britain, France, Denmark, Germany and Sweden. A few of them made use of African slaves in Europe but they were mostly involved in trafficking from Africa to the New World. Those of them with colonies in the New World also made use of slave labour in their possessions.

The U.S.A, many South American countries and the Caribbean states benefited from slave labour. The USA and Brazil were also involved in trafficking from Africa to the New World.

Greece, Turkey and Rome also made extensive use of African slaves.

There is no doubt that many other European and Asian states made use of African slaves on a smaller scale. After all, it has been reported that some of them were found even in China.

The largest concentrations of identifiable true victims of the slave trades are in the USA, the Caribbean and South America. Others are located in Zanzibar and the other islands off the East African Coast. Actually, their descendants exist in one form or the other in all territories that they were ever exported to. Many of them however have been assimilated into the culture and civilisation of their new homelands over the years.

In Africa today, it is almost an impossible task to attempt to locate the surviving families of those who lost their dear ones in the course of the slave trades. It is a lost to the whole continent. The whole continent took part in inflicting the pain and suffering which paradoxically the whole continent is suffering.

What needs to be done by African perpetrators.

There is a lot they can do. These include acceptance of complicity in the past trades, expression of guilt for the present trafficking and slavery, repentance, rendering of apology, putting an end to today's slavery and ensuring good governance.

Africans cannot run away from the truth, especially the truth of their history, which took place in the recent past. The slave trade took place within the historic period. Even if many African communities could not read and write, the Arabs and Europeans who interacted with Africans, documented the African role as well as their roles in sources like travellers' journals, diaries, newspapers and private letters. Many African communities who could not read and write recorded the suffering inflicted on them by African slave raiders in the "fixed-text" type of oral traditions such as drum music, horn music and folk music. There are some Africans still living who occasionally release bits of facts passed on to them by past generations regarding either what they suffered in the hands of African slave raiders, or the wars they fought against others in order to capture them for sale into slavery.

Next, they have to repent. Repentance may be defined as thinking with regret or sorrow regarding an act one performed, and wishing that one had not done so. It is basically a moral word, and it is normally used in relation to sin.

Paul Collins has looked at the concept of repentance within the Christian context.[1] The views he expresses are extremely useful to the whole of humanity. They are certainly pertinent in trying to find a permanent solution to the question of slavery and human trafficking. He starts by making clear WHAT REPENTANCE IS NOT.

1. Not Just Feeling Guilty
2. Not Just Feeling Sorry For Your Sin
3. Not Just Trying To Be A Good Person
4. Not Becoming Religious
5. Not Just Knowing The Truth.

More importantly, TRUE REPENTANCE is
1. Being Sorry To God For Your Sin
2. Being Truthful About Your Sin
3. Turning Away From Your Sin
4. Hating Sin
5. When Possible, Paying Back To Others What You Owe.

Africans have always been a religious people. Before the introduction of foreign religions, every African community

1. R. Mahoney (ed), 1993, (rev.1996), pp. 11. A: 16-17

practised traditional religion in one form or the other. Central to their beliefs, was the existence of God and the creation of man by God. Islam was then introduced into the continent. Many people, especially in East, and Northern Africa as well as the Sudan belt embraced the religion. It also emphasises the existence of God, and the creation of man by Allah. Christianity was also introduced as a universal religion. It has also attracted a very large following especially in West, Central and Southern Africa. Again, it stresses the existence of God and the creation of man in the image of God. All these religions teach that man is the property of God and must live to do His will.

At whatever stage of the history of Africa that Africans sold their fellow human beings, they sold God's property, not theirs. It does not matter that some sections of the Bible and the Koran seemed to permit their adherents to possess slaves. Some other sections talk about loving our neighbours as ourselves, and doing unto others that which we would like them to do unto us; which, when reversed, is that we should not do to others that which we do not want them to do unto us. Africans, whether as traditional practitioners, Muslims or Christians sinned against God at every stage of the processes involved in the enslavement of their neighbours. What the creator requires of sinners is repentance. Now that the truth has dawned on us, we have to feel guilty and sorry. We have to be truthful of the fact that we sold our brothers and sisters for foreign material goods, which were so attractive to us that we could not resist them. We valued them more than our kith and kin. We have to stop further trafficking and slavery. The temptation to do so will never go away - because temptation never goes away. We can however succeed when we accept that slavery is a sin and we resolve to hate it as such.

For true Christians, hating the sin of slavery becomes a matter of course. It is just a matter of turning in faith to God for the strength to do so. Christ solved that problem once and for all on the Cross, on behalf of man. Man only has to accept the completed work of Christ. When man truly turns to God, God is able to turn him to right living.

For Muslims and the practitioners of traditional religion, nobody went to the Cross for them. They nevertheless accept that sin is evil. They also have to accept that slavery is a sin and hate it as such. They have to turn to God the creator, who they worship and depend on Him to turn them to right living.

If possible, the present generation of Africans have to make some form of payment to the true victims of slavery. No direct payment can be made to those who were actually caught and sold to various destinations, or those who died in the process, simply because they are dead. But their living descendants could be compensated. But Africans today are so poor and indebted that they can ill afford to make any financial payment. Ironically, the descendants of slavery in the Diaspora are today better off financially than Africans in the homeland. There is fortunately another form of restitution that works wonders. The poorest of the poor has it to give. It is apology.

Apology is a statement of regret for doing that which is wrong. It is a universal practice that features in every culture. It is intended to attract forgiveness and restore normal relationship between the offended and the offender. The commonest form of its expression is "I am sorry." It may be expressed orally or in the written form or both.

It is not easy to express, because it is perceived as an act of humiliation, which strikes at the very roots of the pride of the person rendering the apology. Secondly, when sincerely rendered, it makes it extremely difficult for the render to commit the same or similar misconduct against the offended.

One other factor that inhibits the rendering of apology is the differences in beliefs and perceptions between individuals and cultural groups regarding what is right and what is wrong. Many African societies, unlike Europeans do not consider certain practices as slavery. A woman may go to work on the farm all day with the child tied to the back. Whilst returning home, she may carry a head load of foodstuff or firewood. At home, she must fetch water and cook the evening meal. Her healthy husband, who just decided not to go to farm that day, and spent the whole day drinking and playing games under shades of trees, must be the first to be served the meal. He must also be served the best part. After the meal, the woman must heat water for the man to bathe. Such a woman is not a slave. She is only a good wife!

Africans need to apologise to the true victims of slavery. Apology is the most effective means of obtaining forgiveness and ensuring harmonious relationship and mutual respect between all parties. The apology must come as the result of the acceptance that slavery and human trafficking is wrong, by the standards of world civilisation, and a sin against God.

Once the apology has been rendered, all African states must take practical steps to stop today's trafficking and slavery. Mere declarations and resolutions will not do. Excuses that other parts of the World are practising it will not do. It does no harm to Africa to be credited with the verdict that it was the first continent to lead in the fight for the eradication of slavery.

Education, both formal and non-formal, is essential. The teachers who are going to be involved in teaching others will themselves have to be made conversant with the United Nations definition of slavery. They will need to know the different forms of slavery that are practised today. Not many people for example know that child labour is a form of slavery. The ILO Convention No. 182 of 1999 however makes it a bedfellow with slavery. It defines the "worst forms of child labour" as "all forms of practices similar to slavery such as the sale and trafficking of children, debt bondage and serfdom and forced labour or compulsory labour including the recruitment of children for use in armed conflict; the use, procurement or offering of a child for prostitution, production of pornography or pornographic performances; the use, procurement or offering of a child for illicit activities, in particular for the production and trafficking of drugs; work which by its nature or circumstances in which it is carried out, is likely to harm the health, safety or morals of children. The Convention also requires states to take account of the special situation of girls and young children." The convention clearly frowns on trafficking of the child and the use of child labour, which is similar to slavery.

The teaching and learning of slavery and other related human rights issues have to be made compulsory but non-examinable subjects for the purpose of awarding certificates in all pre-tertiary schools in Africa. Non-formal education has to be organised for out of school populations. The various forms of mass communication media have to be utilised in informing and educating the people, both in the official languages and in the major local languages.

African states have to put in place the requisite legal and regulatory mechanisms to effectively deal with slavery and human trafficking. Besides the enactment of anti-slavery legislations, there should be the commitment to ensure the enforcement of the laws. In many African countries, many laws are honoured more by their breaching with impunity than by their observance. Ghana boasts of being the first country to ratify the UN Convention on the Rights of the Child, which came into force in September 1990. The country ratified it on 20th November 1989. The convention stipulates the rights of the child as the

- Right to survival
- Right to be protected against harmful influences
- Right to physical, moral and intellectual development
- Right to participate actively in social and cultural life.

It is over 10 years since the ratification took place. Besides the Agencies and Organisations directly involved in Children's Rights and perhaps some other Human rights issues, it is doubtful if other Ghanaians have heard or remember what the Convention is about. It is also doubtful if ratification has made impact on a significant number of Ghanaian children.

Awareness creation measures should be introduced. Where they have already been introduced, they should be intensified. Law enforcement agencies should be committed to ensure the success of the laws. The police, immigration authorities and members of the 'Judiciary must all co-operate to apprehend offenders and mete out appropriate punishments. The informed citizenry must also look out for those engaged in trafficking and slavery and report them to the appropriate authorities for the law to take its course.

It is essential that some mechanism is put in place to measure the progress that the African countries are making towards the elimination of human trafficking and slavery. They cannot be their own judges. Fortunately, the United Nations has agencies that can do the monitoring. However, it cannot do it alone. Fortunately there are many reputable NGOs that are already at work in dealing with Human Rights issues in Africa. The African states, the NGOs and the United Nations can come to an agreement on the territories to be covered by each of the approved NGOs. The parties must work in the spirit of trust and co-operation. Any disagreements between the three parties must be resolved in the spirit of co-operation. Together, the battle would be won.

There must be rewards and punishments. The developed countries of the world must offer co-operative states of Africa the various forms of assistance that Africa needs from them to improve their economies and the lot of the people. Sanctions must be imposed on non-co-operative states. Nations the world over, are beginning to realise the damaging effects of sanctions either from the UN or from the powerful states of the world, particularly the USA. South Africa felt it in the Apartheid era. Libya felt it over the Lockerbie affair. Iraq is hurting under the Weapons inspection issue. Afghanistan, under the Taleban regime has just experienced it. Perhaps what the world needs to experience more is the benefits of co-operation.

Good governance is needed to liberate people from slavery conditions and to end pushing others out of Africa into slavery conditions.

The United Nations, the Commonwealth and the Organisation of African Unity (now called the African Union) have gone a long way in curbing the imposition of both military and civilian dictatorships, on the citizens of African countries. However, there is still much to be done to improve the political situation in almost all African countries. Incumbent political parties want to hold on to power at all cost. The opposition parties also want to unseat the government at all cost. Elections in all African countries are preceded by accusations and counter accusations of intended irregularities. It has become the order of the day for external monitors to be involved in the elections in African countries. Even then, there are still post election accusations of irregularities directed at the incumbent political parties, which invariably win the election. African governments have a lot to do to promote confidence in the electoral system.

The winner takes all phenomenon has to be eliminated. Appointments in public services, award of government contracts, etc. are given only to government party members.

It is very easy to predict the verdict of cases in court between the government or government party officials and those in opposition. This happens despite the theoretical declaration of the independence of the judiciary.

The choice for people without much conscience is to always cross over to the government parties. To those with sensitive consciences, the only option is to exit from their countries if they want to make an honest living. There are many talented and professional Africans in the Diaspora who emigrated for these reasons. This brain drain adversely affects the development of Africa.

It contributes to the perpetuation of poverty in Africa, which also contributes to slavery and human trafficking in Africa. Again, some of these professionals and other talented people are never able to secure employment in the host countries in their fields of specialisation. They are forced to take on some undesirable jobs, just so that they can earn a living. Stories have been told of some engineers, chemists and even some medical doctors who have been forced to take to the driving of taxis because of this situation. Such people continue to live under mental slavery.

Because of the inter-territorial nature of the problem, there must be greater co-operation between the countries of Africa to put an end to the cross-border trafficking. Their immigration and law enforcement agencies must co-ordinate their measures and schemes geared towards combating human trafficking.

African governments must co-operate in their bid to identify victims of the slave trade in their countries and repatriate them to their countries of origin. All the countries should institute rehabilitation schemes to assist returnees to adjust to the normal life. Actually, the Nigerian government has already moved in this direction. It launched a presidential Task Force on August 23, 2001 for this purpose.[2] What is more important than the launching is ensuring that the task force performs effectively.

All the efforts directed at stopping human trafficking and slavery will come to nought if African governments do not take measures to radically improve upon their economies. No legislation can stop the poverty stricken masses from reacting in undesirable ways, including releasing their children to traffickers, who deceive them into believing that such transactions will bring improvement to both the child and the parents. Internal economic hardships will continue to drive educated and uneducated, professional and non-professionals into foreign countries in search of greener pastures. Many of these people will continue to end up in slavery conditions in their host countries. They constitute an unwanted people and they sometimes end up in jail as illegal immigrants or criminals. Perhaps, it is high time that African governments and private companies emulated John H. Johnson, who is acclaimed by many people as the most powerful African-American businessman in the USA. He founded the "Negro Digest" and "Ebony". He used a special but common motivational technique to stop the brain drain or poaching from his Enterprise, which was near to collapsing because of this problem. He made up a list of thirty employees he must retain at all cost. He gave them all they needed. None of them left until retirement or death. He grew them and they grew his businesses.[3] Most public and private sector employers pay slave wages to their

---

2. Anti-Slavery "reporter", Oct 2001, p. 4
3. P. Krass (ed), 1998, p. 294

African workers because the enterprises are poor. The demoralised workers pretend to be working and the employers continue to pretend to be paying the workers. The result is that both the enterprises and the workers continue to be poor. The unfortunate part is that many of the best brains and the daring ones move out to offer their services to the developed countries.

There are many unemployed people with skills on the streets of African cities. Some of them could start their own small-scale businesses with a little help. The help needed is mainly some basic entrepreneurship training and some small loan to be used as capital. Such people should be identified and assisted. Without any assistance, frustration sets in. Some of the frustrated ones could easily end up as human traffickers. Then also, some especially the female ones could end up as victims of trafficking and slavery. It is such people who are usually lured into prostitution, both in and outside Africa.

African governments also need to initiate or intensify Family Planning schemes. High birth rates of poverty stricken rural communities and the unemployed or low-income earners of the cities constitute a setback to any attempt to combat trafficking and slavery. Such people who have eight or more children are eager to offload some of the "children of burden" to traffickers who specialise in deceiving the parents with promises. Some of the parents are also compelled to use their children to perform slavery tasks to ensure the survival of the household. Even for the poor, smaller families will reduce their poverty or their burden of having to feed and clothe more people. The smaller the number of children, the greater the chances of the parents of braving the odds to offer them basic formal education to equip them with the skills needed to fend for themselves in future.

Certain cultural practices have to be abolished. They constitute discrimination and slavery, even though nobody is condemning them. One of them is the institutionalised treatment given to the ruling class by some designated lineage members. On some special occasions, the chiefs must be carried around durbar grounds. About four people must carry the palanquins on their heads with the chief dancing and stomping in them. There is no room for making a mistake that may result in the palanquin and the chief falling down. In the olden days, the carriers would certainly be beheaded. Today, it is not known what would be done. But something would certainly be done. The sad aspect is that the would-be carrier, once designated, has no right to refuse to perform the duty.

Somehow, African governments must embark on some form of education that liberates the minds of people from their obsession for foreign goods, and the disposition to reject every locally manufactured good. The reason commonly given has to do with the quality. Quality however, can only improve with usage, practice and more research. Entrepreneurs will buy research findings and go into production to create more jobs and incomes only when they know that there is market for their products. Without the growth in local production and productivity, the unemployment and poverty will persist. This does not augur well for the successful elimination of human trafficking and slavery. Unless the obsession with foreign goods is curbed, the unscrupulous unemployed or low income earner with irresistible desire for foreign cars and electronic gadgets for example could be tempted into making adventure into human trafficking and related vices for making quick money.

What needs to be done by the generality of Africans

The attitude and behaviour of Africans suggest that they consider themselves to be distinct and separate from their governments. They vote their representatives into office. Beyond that, the majority of people confine themselves to thinking and dealing with issues that directly affect themselves and members of their families.

However, for the problems of the past and present human trafficking and slavery to be dealt with successfully, there is the need for the involvement of every single individual. After all, when every individual says No to slavery, the problem is solved. But when governments, International Organisations, and NGOs say No but individuals say YES, the problem cannot be solved - not even under dictatorships.

Individuals must repent of their actions after they have been conscientised. They must even feel sorry and show remorse for the sins of their ancestors and their present neighbours even when they themselves are not practising it.

Every individual needs to apologise to the true victims of slavery.

This must be followed by the decision to eschew human trafficking, slavery and other illegal or immoral economic activities.

The person not engaged in the malpractices must assume the responsibility of influencing his guilty neighbour or friend to give it up. This may even necessitate his reporting him to the law enforcement agencies for arrest and prosecution if he is recalcitrant. The police, immigration personnel and other law enforcement agencies have to discharge their duties conscientiously and avoid the temptation to collude with the offenders to the embarrassment of informants.

Then, every individual must resolve to do an honest job. Those without any requisite skills must acquire the skills needed to enable them start some productive venture. Every enterprise, no matter how small its beginnings, can be grown into a big and prosperous one with determination and dedication.

Every individual must reject those cultural practices that are suggestive of slavery or bondage. These include carrying chiefs in palanquins, a woman who is given a small sum of money, or less than ten cows as her dowry and is expected to be responsible for the upkeep of her husband and children for the rest of her life. The husband is exempted from providing any money for housekeeping after paying the dowry.

What needs to be done by foreign perpetrators

None of the Western developed countries which took part in the slave trade or benefited from it has so far denied responsibility for her involvement. They have however refused to be part of a forum that aims at making them accept sole responsibility for the trade. Perhaps they have been trying to avoid the inevitable embarrassment that their defence would create for their accusers - especially the African accusers; "You were equally guilty, if not more guilty than us."

It is now time for all parties to be candid, if the embarrassing issue is to be buried once and for all. The targeted developed countries of the West, and the Arab and Asian states must all accept responsibility.

They must all make the open declaration that they acted wrongly. All must express regret at their involvement and resolve that never again will they and their descendants involve themselves in slave trade and slavery.

They must watch out for the various forms it is practised in their countries today and strive to stamp it out. They must work at its eradication - the enslavement of man by man.

The foreigners must also render open apology to the true victims of the slave trade and slavery. The apology must go to the living descendants as well as the past generations. They must also apologise to those in slavery and other forms of bondage conditions in their countries and work towards their emancipation. They must apprehend and punish today's beneficiaries of slaves and the traffickers in their countries.

They must initiate or support measures and schemes aimed at reducing poverty, corruption, etc. which are some of the main underlying causes of slavery, the slave trade and other illegal economic activities. The level of aid they give to African countries should be contingent upon evidence of commitment and co-operation of the countries in ensuring the success of the exercise.

In a spirit of sympathy, the foreign countries could even launch a sort of "Marshall Plan" for Africa. Africa could do with a little help from her friends, not as a matter of right but in the spirit of co-operation and unity.

What needs to be done by the true victims:

There is no doubt that the true victims of slavery are entitled to incalculable emotional and material compensation. No material compensation will ever wipe away or reduce their humiliation and suffering. Besides, the direct victims are dead and gone.

The noblest thing that they can do at this stage of history is to accept the sincere apology of the world in general and the perpetrators in particular. Having accepted the apology, they have to forgive Africa, which betrayed them. They have to forgive the foreigners who kept them in captivity and debased and abused them. They have to thank God that the worst is over, and be grateful to the powers that be that their powerful tormentors have had their consciences tormented and have sought their freedom though repentance and apology. They must derive satisfaction from the irony that they have become the ultimate liberators.

They could extend a hand of friendship to Africa to help her get out of the chronic poverty pervading the continent. They have acquired useful technology, skills and wealth in the Diaspora that could be used to transform Africa. Perhaps their experience is similar to that of Joseph and his brothers. They sold him into slavery in the land of Egypt. But it was Joseph who saved them from perishing during the great famine. His words in Gen. 45:5 speak it all: "Now therefore be not grieved, nor angry with yourselves, that ye sold me hither: for God did send me before you to preserve life."

What needs to be done by the U.N

The United Nations Organisation is the only Organisation that embraces all the nations of the world. It has a critical role to play in resolving the issue of reparations for slavery. Once it has taken a definite stand that is acceptable to the parties involved, the matter would be considered to have been settled for the world for eternity. Until this is done the problem will linger on. It is significant that it demonstrated its awareness of the responsibility that rests on her by organising the World Conference Against Racism, Racial Discrimination, Xenophobia and Related Intolerance in Durban, South Africa, through its Commission for Human Rights. It is now obvious that the conference did not succeed in solving the problem to the satisfaction of the opposing factions; the perceived beneficiaries of slavery and the perceived victims of slavery (the western developed nations and Africa).

The UN has to organise the world, particularly the two divides to refocus their attention on the problem. There must be genuine introspection and an objective reassessment of the roles played by all. All, particularly the claimants of compensation must be encouraged to accept that the issue at stake is not reparations, but the eradication of slavery.

The UN must create a forum for former White, Arab and Asian buyers and African sellers to apologise for their crime. Having apologised, the UN must also apologise on behalf of all of humanity to the true victims.

The world body must then erect a memorial to the true victims. The memorial must also remind the world of the new understanding that genuine apology has been rendered and accepted, and the civilised world has resolved that never again will it happen. In addition to the erection of a physical commemorative monument, a special UN day marking the end of slavery may be instituted.

The world needs friendship, peace and unity based on apology and forgiveness. The UN can and must rally the nations of the world towards the attainment of this goal.

BIBLIOGRAPHY

Ajayi, J. K. and Espie, I (eds) (1969) A Thouand Years of West African History (Ibadan; University of Ibadan Press and London; Thomas Nels on and Sons Ltd

Akosah-Sarpong, Kofi (2001) "The coming trial of discrimination" WEST AFRICA 4290 27th August p19

Anene, J.C. and Brown, G. (eds) 1966) Africa in the Nineteenth and Twentieth Centuries (Ibadan: University of Ibadan Press and London: Thomas Nelson and Sons Ltd)

Authorised King James Version (1986) Holy Bible (IOWA: World Bible Publishers)

Boahen, A. A. with Ajayi, J. F. A and Tidy, M (1988) Topics in West African History (Essex: Longman Group Ltd)

Buah, F. K. (1979) History Notes: West Africa since AD 2000 (London, MacMillan)

Duodu, Cameron. (2001) "Reparations: proper debate needed" WEST AFRICA 4290 27th August pp20-22

Fynn, J.K. and Addo-Fening, R with Anquandah, J. (1991) History For Senior Secondary Schools (London: Evans Brothers Ltd and Accra: Ministry of Education)

Grandreams Ltd, (1996) The Concise Encyclopedia (London: Grandreams Ltd)

Gyan-Apenteng, Kwasi. (2001) "Durban and beyond" WEST AFRICA 4293 17th September p12

Gyan-Apenteng, Kwasi (2001) "Compromise and achievement" WEST AFRICA 4293 17th September p14

Kelty, M. G (1937) The story of the American People (Boston: The Athenaeum Press)

Krass, Peter (ed) (1998) The Book of Leadership Wisdom (John Wiley & Sons)

Mohoney, R. (ed) (1993) The Shepherd's Staff, India Edition (Burbank: World MAP)

Microsoft® Encarta® 98 Encyclopedia © 1993-1997 Microsoft Corp "Holocaust"

Ogot, B. A. (ed) (1992) General History of Africa. V, Africa from the Sixteenth to the Eighteenth Century (Berkeley: University of California Press)

Shillington, K. (1989) History of Africa (London and Basingstoke: MACMILLAN EDUCATION LTD)

Webster, J: B. and Boahen, A.A. with Idowu H.O. (1967) The Growth of African Civilization The Revolutionary Years (London: Longmans Group Ltd)

World Book, Inc (1992) The World Book Encyclopedia B Vol 2

World Book Encyclopedia (1985) USA: World Book Inc.)

Printed in the United States
by Baker & Taylor Publisher Services